FIRM BELIEFS

INSIGHTS THAT MATTER FOR TOMORROW'S LEADER

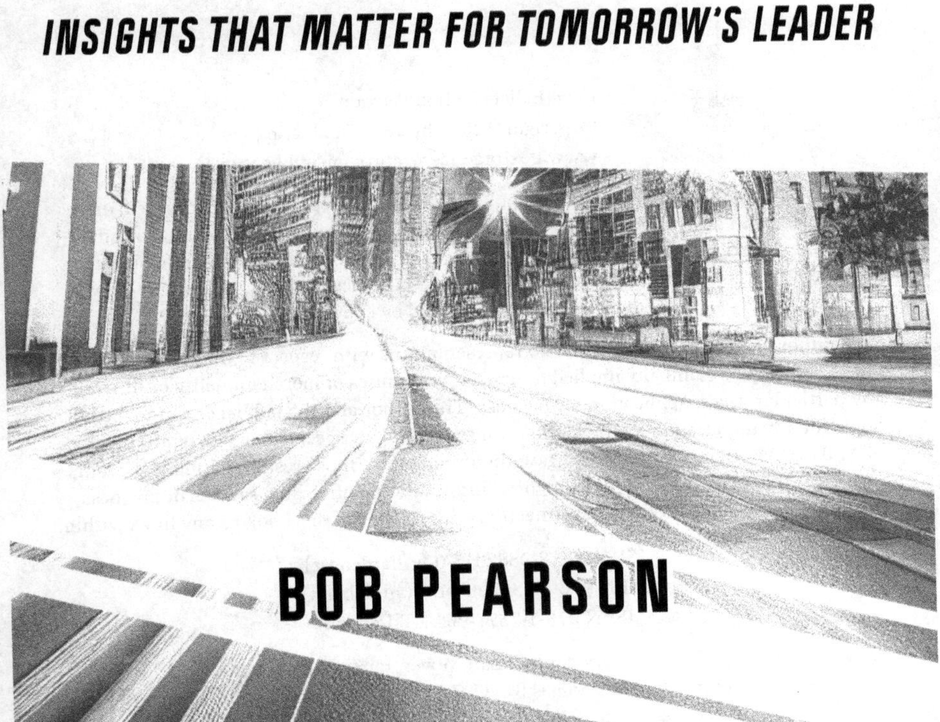

BOB PEARSON

Books by Bob Pearson

Pre-Commerce

Storytizing

Countering Hate
with Haroon K. Ullah

Crafting Persuasion
with Kip Knight and Ed Tazzia

Firm Beliefs by Bob Pearson

www.nextpracticesgroup.com/publications

ISBN 979-8-9882315-0-9 (hardcover)
ISBN 978-1-7377964-1-1 (audiobook)
ISBN 978-1-7377-964-2-8 (e-book)

Editorial services by Misti Moyer, mistimoyer.com
Book design by Monica Thomas for TLC Book Design,TLCBookDesign.com
Cover photo © Cary Peterson for Adobe Stock.com

My first "coaches" in life taught me how to learn forever after.

Thank you Mom and Dad

TABLE OF CONTENTS

INNOVATION

PERSONAL GROWTH

INTRODUCTION

FIRM BELIEFS— WHY IT WAS WRITTEN

We all have read academic books and papers that tell us how our world works. In these models, everything works just right.

We all know this isn't the case, since real life is never so neat.

Let's face it. We're human, and humans are on an endless journey to figure out how to calibrate their own personalities, expertise, and experience with those of others to come up with solutions we all desire. We're more complicated than we may think, particularly when you put hundreds of us together to accomplish common goals.

It's the definition of imperfect.

We all know this, which is why we spend so much time coaching each other and outlining how we work, what our expectations are, and why an old model still works or needs to get blown up.

It's this journey that we reflect on in *Firm Beliefs*.

What I realized when I was a twenty-two-year-old kid who just joined his first consulting firm was that the more senior people sure made a lot of sense. They seemed to know things I thought were epiphanies. Of course, they weren't.

What it was, however, was powerful. It's the collective wisdom of their careers.

It's also something that is rarely gathered into one place.

Firm Beliefs is a collection of a lifetime of learning, all focused on how to build the best firm or team in the business.

Not a single idea is a big one or a breakthrough, which is part of the point.

The most successful firms are like the best teams in sports or entertainment. We say they have "great chemistry" or "they make it look easy."

When you dig deeper, you see that they may be very smart or proficient in their specific jobs, but what really drives success is an unrelenting focus on getting it right and being a team player while doing it.

Firm Beliefs is an apt name for a very simple reason: Each observation or insight is time-tested. These same observations and insights are often built on a series of failed experiments that sounded great, but never worked.

The good news is that there is plenty of room for the next great firm to emerge for an equally simple reason: Most of us don't take the time to think through all the details of becoming a great firm. We say it is due to our workload ("I work so hard!"), we say we'll do it next quarter ("once things slow down"), or we just assume our personal brilliance will carry the day.

This book is written to guide those on the path to greatness.

Enjoy, and let me know what you believe should be added. It's a journey that never ends.

LEADERSHIP

CHAPTER 1

WISDOM FROM GLOBAL LEADERS

"It is the province of knowledge to speak,
but it is the privilege of wisdom to listen."

—*Oliver Wendell Holmes*

You wake up in the middle of the night and wonder if what you are doing is right or if you missed an important point. Are you making the right calls? Do you have the right leaders in the right places? What could I be doing wrong (or right)?

If we are honest, every entrepreneur has these moments. Maybe not every night, but we've all had them.

I have been blessed to watch top global CEOs in action, often when few others are looking.

It is this wisdom that I share in this chapter and throughout the book.

Here are a few moments that have stayed with me forever:

Let us start with Ed Meyer, who began in account services in 1956 and rose to become CEO of Grey Global Group in 1970. He took a $29.5 million firm and built it into a $1.3 billion firm in 2003 with operations in eighty countries. Ed has always been known as one of the most client-focused CEOs in the advertising business.

In a free moment, I asked him, "How do you know when to open a new office?"

He gave me a look that reflected how simple this answer was. He said everything is client driven. When clients need us in a new geography, we start the office. When we hear their needs, we build the new offering before they officially ask for it. That is it.

Great leaders can see the future more clearly because they listen with intent every day.

Great leaders can see the future more clearly because they listen with intent every day.

Rob Cawthorn became president of Rorer in 1984. Five years later, he formed Rhône-Poulenc Rorer, now known as Sanofi, one of the top global pharmaceutical companies on the planet.

Rob is a gentleman and a dealmaker extraordinaire. He loved shaping the future of the company and had the audacity to imagine little, tiny Rorer could evolve into a global pharma company at a time when most people would have probably told him he was dreaming too much.

Sitting in Rob's conference room one day working on an announcement, I noticed him pick up the phone and call the exact person who might have an answer. He would skip layers and go right to the accounting manager or the product manager rather than their boss.

Rob explained this approach, and I realized he really had two objectives. The first was that he wanted the answer quickly and had a distaste for bureaucracy. The second is there is no way he could keep up with all the details of the company, but if everyone thought he could, everyone raised their game, since no one wanted to get a call and not be ready.

In another conference room moment, we were working full speed at the end of the year as many were starting to relax for the holidays. We were about to sell the most iconic brand Rorer had created, which Rhône-Poulenc Rorer now owned, Maalox. We sold it to CIBA-GEIGY on December 22, 1994.

At the time, I was having trouble accepting we would sell it because everyone knew the brand.

While working on the news release, I said, "Rob, Maalox is so important to the history of Rorer. Why are you selling it?"

Rob looked at me with a slight smile and said, "Bob, we are getting excellent value for Maalox, that's why."

I walked away, knowing he was right. Rob was willing to sell a brand associated with the history of his past company and take any flack, so he could fund the development of his new firm, Rhône-Poulenc Rorer. We were doing clinical trials for what would become the leading cancer drug (Taxotere), the first-ever drug for ALS (Rilutek), and the most important US launch in the company's history (Lovenox).

Rob saw all of this clearly and realized Maalox would fund our future. It took a minute for me to wipe the history from my brain before I could see it as clearly as he could.

Great leaders can think clearly in the moment.

Great leaders can think clearly in the moment.

Dan Vasella is a medical doctor who rose through the ranks in Sandoz and became the first CEO of Novartis, when CIBA-GEIGY and Sandoz merged in 1996. Dan transformed the two companies during his fourteen-year tenure as CEO, creating a leading global pharma powerhouse.

When you build a company like Novartis, it is easy to get press. It is easy to speak where you want. The world is coming at you. You really pick and choose your moments. And this is where I learned a lesson from Dan I will never forget. It impacted me both professionally and personally.

On December 26, 2004, a major tsunami created death and destruction in the countries in and around the Indian Ocean. Dan immediately led efforts to bring medicines to faraway lands, such as Sri Lanka, fly doctors to places in need, and provide any other support we could. It was urgent and inspirational, and our commitment was immediately for the long term.

Dan and I were talking about the work, and he thought I was ready to push for an announcement of our efforts. He was probably right since I was known for communicating about everything I could. He looked at me and pointedly said, "We are not going to thump our chest like the other companies. No announcement. We just do the work."

So, at a time when it seemed every company was touting their efforts, Dan chose to say nothing and focus on delivering care.

Great leaders believe history is their judge, not today's headline.

It was really a parable of why we were working in a pharmaceutical company. Despite the criticisms of the industry, we all just kept moving, since we knew who we were helping. That is what drove us every day. That is purpose-driven work.

Great leaders believe history is their judge, not today's headline.

CHAPTER 2

THE POWER OF QUESTIONS

"Management teams aren't good at asking questions.
In business school, we train them to be good at giving answers."
—*Clayton M. Christensen*

Clayton M. Christensen was walking off the stage after keynoting at a business conference, and I stood up and walked to the side of the stage to say hello.

He was a leading thinker in the academic and business world who developed the famous "disruptive innovation theory," which outlines the importance of recognizing a new market at its earliest stage before competitors do the same and, in particular, how to recognize when new competitors will enter at the bottom of a market and eventually displace established leaders.

Like how Netflix created the streaming market.

Or how Kia became a leading carmaker in the US.

I told Clayton I worked at Dell, and he immediately started talking about how the technology industry was making significant moves towards software, services, and storage and why companies like ours needed to move with more speed in this direction. Back in the early 2000s, this thinking was still being challenged, believe it or not. But Clayton had trained himself to routinely find the new paths that would form and disrupt or expand markets.

He was right, of course.

Meeting him and learning what he had to say stuck with me, since this type of ability centered around asking powerful questions.

It is not just listening. It is not just asking questions. It is about asking *powerful* questions that cause us to think and act differently.

Looking back at my career, I realize that the best CEOs I have worked and interacted with are all great at asking the types of questions that make you walk away thinking, "Why didn't I think of that?"

Michael Dell is, in my view, the best at this skill I have ever seen. In a story I have told many times, I had mentioned to Michael that we needed to develop a response policy for any complaint we found online and commit to a timeframe. He agreed and set me off to do this. I returned after collaborating with a team of expert colleagues to show him a policy committing us to respond to any online complaint within twenty-four hours.

Michael reviewed the policy and had one edit and one question: "Bob, I believe you made a typo." I asked, "Where?" "You are missing a period between the two and the four." I laughed and said that would be hard to do, but ok, we'll do it. He then asked, "Why did you not start from zero and work from there?"

It is a question I have never forgotten. I was so focused on achieving group consensus that we ended up at twenty-four hours, yet it would have been more appropriate and customer-focused to start at zero and see how much time we really needed to respond.

That question changed our policy, and it has made me question bureaucracy in new ways ever since.

That is a powerful question.

For all of us, how can we ask more powerful questions?

Here are some common things I have learned from those who ask powerful questions:

The best questioners relentlessly study their firm, industry, and trends to keep a perpetual edge in being "street smart." Whether it is clients, new customers, financial information, products, or any topic related to their business, they are experts due to their intense focus. They have a view that is expansive, not insular.

Leaders realize they can tell you to get a job done and you will, but an answer *we discover ourselves* can change our habits for the long term. Their goal is to get us to understand what we are either doing incorrectly or not at all so we can course correct. They don't believe in giving orders. They believe in changing our mindset.

The questions are very direct. You understand their question but maybe cannot answer it on the spot. In fact, if you can always answer questions on the spot, then you are either being asked softball questions or your leader isn't very good at challenging you.

You don't always feel comfortable when being asked the question. Their goal is not to make you feel good. Their goal is to make you realize what you could and should consider doing. The key is not to take it personally.

It takes a real commitment to be a perpetual learner and to make time to form powerful questions.

Many leaders equate the "speed" of their reaction with caring. This certainly keeps the wheels moving, but it doesn't open minds.

Great leaders also work hard and move fast, but they are always thinking about what questions they can ask their leaders to set them free and make a larger difference in the firm.

Imagine the top ten leaders in your firm. What question do you want to ask them over the next few weeks that would help them see new value in changing their behavior? If you don't have a question in mind, why? What is holding you back as a leader?

The usual response is that you are too busy. So how is it that CEOs of companies with one hundred thousand people and over $100 billion in revenue can find time to ask powerful questions? You know this is an excuse.

If you are a CEO or lead a key C-suite function, ask yourself the type of question Clayton would have asked you.

What new opportunity in your area of expertise is opening up, and what is your plan? Remember, it's unlikely to be so obvious that

everyone is doing it. Your goal is to lead the herd, not follow it.

Where are the weakest areas of your firm, and what are you doing to strengthen them?

If you develop the ability to ask your team powerful questions, it is a sign that you are being thoughtful about how you build your firm.

Try it and see if you can ask those questions without providing the answer right away.

CHAPTER 3

THE THREE DRIVERS OF A CHIEF EXECUTIVE OFFICER'S NARRATIVE

"If you can dream it, you can do it."

— *Walt Disney*

A chief executive officer's world is a chaotic one.

There is the pressure from investors and shareholders. The intensity of putting points on the board every day and quarter. The need to invest in the future while you maintain proper cash flow. An employee base that is asking for your full attention.

It is a list of important areas that are a mile long.

Then we come in.

Sometimes we make the mistake of saying, "So, what do you want to talk about for the next year?"

The CEO can quickly discount this type of question. After all, they have already planned out their exact actions for the next twelve months, have a three- or five-year plan, and are in execution mode.

It's the wrong question to ask.

What a CEO is looking to do is inspire their teams to do more than they thought was possible. To work with an urgency that will separate them from competitors. And to do this as a team.

Inspiring CEO-driven narratives can sound different, but they have three fundamental drivers.

Here are the three ingredients we find that lead to the most productive discussions:

How will your market evolve over the next five years? The CEO is the narrator of how our marketplace will change over five years. They have insights others do not. Facts we have not yet heard. Great CEOs take the time to educate us on what's ahead.

What new products and services will you introduce during this time? Our R&D efforts are directly aligned with our future. The importance of us building new products and services makes sense in context with how the market is evolving. We see our R&D colleagues as our agents of change.

How can your team make a difference in your journey? We feel an urgency to step up our game every day to improve how we work, as individuals and teams, so we can achieve our mission. We realize that we don't have time to waste. Our customers need us!

The actual narrative aligns with these three drivers of our story.

The CEO and their team are planning for a future that will require urgency, innovation, and teamwork. It should be inspiring and clear if it is to build the trust and confidence critical to matching words with results.

It's our job to ensure the CEO's dream becomes a reality.

CHAPTER 4

THE MENTALITY OF A LEADING FIRM

"Never say never, because limits, like fears, are often just an illusion."

—*Michael Jordan*

You know the feeling.

You are working hard at the office, but you are waiting for that phone call. The phone rings, and you hear, "We really like your team and hope we can work together, but you didn't win the assignment."

We know why clients tell us this. Partly because they believe it and partly because they don't want us to feel bad, since they are nice people.

If they really liked us, the other agency would have received the call.

What matters is how you react to this situation. It's what separates the top firm from the rest.

If you ask leaders about their mentality, like Michael Jordan or Tom Brady, they essentially say:

They always imagine how they will win.

They always assume they are on the right team and deserve to win.

And in between games, they are driven by an inner voice that tells them to practice harder, study plays more intensely, motivate their teammates more, and to never accept excuses.

It is very translatable to our business.

We practice by doing work for our clients every day. We learn both by doing and by reading relentlessly outside of work. When asked what the most important thing he does to succeed in business, Warren Buffett has consistently said that he reads constantly. It's not just work.

We know it is incumbent on us to help our teammates be strong, so we are at our best. Individuals who are great cannot carry a team. A team carries a team. Leaders coach their teammates since they want everyone to excel.

Leaders seek out feedback. They desire constructive criticism. The best coaches deliver it.

And when we lose, we do take it a bit personally. We obsess over what we could have done differently and then fix it. It could be hiring additional people who are talented in new areas or change how we present or something else. But we do not let it go until we understand what it is, and then we fix it. We cannot walk around knowing that we could be the best, but are choosing not to be. Not an option.

The good news for those who care is that most of our competitors are quite satisfied with their status quo. They feel validated to hear they came in second and feel a warmth that the client likes them. They put up an invisible shield that prevents too much introspection. It protects our ego.

Top leaders find a way to lead. They expect to be your top choice every time. And that is why their percentage of success will always be higher. When you have the mentality of a leader, you really do care more and actually do something about it.

LEADERSHIP INSIGHT

Breakdowns Really Do Lead to Breakthroughs

We presented our ideas to launch a new drug, the thirteenth non-steroidal anti-inflammatory drug to enter the US market, to the Voltaren marketing team. Not exactly optimal conditions.

The head of marketing listened to our team's plan and said, "This is not acceptable. We need big ideas. You have until next week to come back with the right plan."

We brainstormed and realized Mickey Mantle could be a great spokesperson. Bad knees, famous athlete, under publicized. I hopped on a plane to Joplin, Missouri, and asked Mickey if he would join our clinical trials. He did, the drug worked, and Mickey became our spokesperson.

A week later, we walked into the same room and unveiled our big idea. We showed a picture of Mickey on the big screen then played an audio recording I made of Mickey talking directly to the head of marketing and his team on why he would like to join us as we handed out signed baseballs to each person.

Fast forward. We launched and became the second-largest drug in the market in six months.

Every breakdown has the chance to turn into a breakthrough. It is all a matter of how we handle the situation.

CHAPTER 5

DON'T LET POWER FORM IN THE WRONG PLACES

"Organizations have to have continuity, and yet if there is not enough new challenge, not enough change, they become empty bureaucracies, awfully fast."

—Peter Drucker

The big question revolves around how we define "power." In my experience, "power" is an asset granted to you by your clients. After all, it is the client who chooses to work with us. It is the client who chooses to fund our work. And it is the client who decides if we continue year after year in partnership.

This makes our decision-making process extra simple.

Will our decisions lead to actions and results that improve our relationship? Will they add value to our workflow? Will they make our firm stronger for the future so that it benefits our clients?

This is the lens to review our ideas to improve the firm.

The most successful consulting firms in the world built global networks based on how to best serve their clients.

So, why do we make it so hard on ourselves? Well, we tend to let power form in the wrong places for the wrong reasons, even if it is not obvious at the start.

In looking for signs of misalignment, I've found five key areas that serve as potential flags with advice on how to deal with each situation.

#1 – One person decides for all. This is the leader who is often the founder. They decide everything, right down to the bonus for admins. No detail is too small. This is a person and firm that is running a business for the benefit of the founder, not its clients. What we do here is form teams. An executive committee of three to four people. A senior leadership team. A team representing entry level to account supervisors. We clarify decision-making by group, and we democratize how we do it.

#2 – Non-client-facing leaders expand their remit for too long. I don't mean finance, HR, IT. I mean when leaders want to form and run new committees that give them broader responsibility. It's fine to set up the equivalent of SWAT teams to figure out a key area for the firm that may impact all its team members, for example. But put an end date on each committee. Ensure that all committees end, and that new people and new ideas get a chance to join the next opportunity. Is anyone really glad that a committee goes on perpetually? Not really.

#3 – We try to please everyone. When we continually pivot a firm to please everyone, we please no one. Consulting firms love to compete on who gives more time off or work schedules or yoga classes and on and on. Any of these activities could be fun and useful. Just keep in mind that firms do not become world-class firms because they offer what everyone wants in the moment, which always changes. Firms that are the best are consistently great at developing the right outcomes for their clients. The key is to listen and evolve, but don't try to please everyone. You never will.

#4 – We favor billability over 5.0 scores. Internally driven firms talk about billability and profitability, and that's about it. Great firms also talk about billability and profitability, but they live for a 5.0 score (1-5) for their client work, based on client input. The 4.5 to 5.0 land of client service will lead to sustainable growth with your clients. A team that is highly billable but running under 3.5 will have less success. Internal bosses often derive too much power from tracking every number and forget the most important number to track, celebrate, and learn from is reaching a 5.0 level of client service.

#5 – We allow power vacuums to exist. You know the drill. Two senior leaders don't like each other, so they don't partner. Two practices are competitive and don't look to mashup their services to deliver better value for their client. Other leaders quietly complain about any other person or group they interact with. All these scenarios are mini power vacuums that cannot be allowed if you want to succeed.

Senior leaders don't have to love each other, but they do need to find out how they and their teams can work together. Practices need to leverage skills of other practices, so a technology and health team show up together and wow the client. And those quiet complainers are like a sniffle that can turn into the flu. Help them get healthy and focus on how to partner and succeed.

We end with this last example for a reason. Often, small pockets of distrust lead to power vacuums, which can lead to what many refer to as politics. Then, as leaders who are associated with these politics gain more responsibility, they actually lose more people in the firm, since they were never fully trusted.

Keep it simple.

Make all decisions, internal and external, to provide the most value to our clients.

Demand that our team members always do the same and work through any issues to persevere on behalf of our clients.

Clarify decision-making, don't bottle it up.

And stay focused on delivering 5.0-level work.

When we stay this focused, it's remarkable how easy it is to make decisions, large and small.

It leads to a dynamic organization that won't tolerate bureaucratic tendencies that keep it from being the best.

CHAPTER 6

AVOID EXCUSES—EMBRACE THE ITERATION OF SUCCESS

"Success is not final. Failure is not fatal.
It is the courage to continue that counts."

—*unknown*

In chapter 4, we discuss the mentality of a leading firm. Let's explore this further using new business, something we all engage in to grow our firms, as an example.

You get a call from a potential client, and they tell you, "We loved your team. Your thinking was great, but we decided to go with another firm. You just missed."

Too often, the receiver of this call then informs their team that they were great. Everything was good; we just didn't win, but we could have.

Here is what I hear when this message comes across:

"Blah, blah, blah…blah, blah, blah…"

A leader simply parroting these warm words to let us down gently is the wrong response. When I was a client, I called it the "velvet glove." Basically, our goal client-side was to never hurt the feelings of an agency who tried hard to win, since we may very well collaborate with them or some of their team in the future. But in that moment, they were not the best. We just didn't feel a need to be that direct.

Science and technology evolve through iteration, which means that each "failure" is actually a learning experience. Breakthroughs occur when we learn from each failure until we create a new solution.

It should be that way in a firm.

So, the next time you get this call, it is ok to repeat what you heard, but then continue with a postmortem with your team to ask yourself, candidly, how you did.

Here is a list I like to use:

#1 – How powerful was our story? If we sent our slide deck to a team who knew nothing about this client, would they be able to read it and understand exactly what we were communicating? Or did the slides not really hang together well?

#2 – How well did we address the client's needs? What exactly would we have done that was unique and better than any other firm? Or did we not go there?

#3 – Did we present with the best team? Did our A team present, or did we go with who was available? Did we bring in leaders from other parts of our firm to up our expertise, or did we keep it more insular to our group?

#4 – How did we manage the full process? How did we handle our first call? What level of questions did we provide during the RFP process to show what we know? Did we bring any handouts to the meeting? Were we all in person? How did we follow up? How did we price? How well did we match our team with the client team for day-to-day management?

If you answer these questions honestly, you see very clearly what you could have done better and how to improve next time. If you review and determine that you did everything correctly, well then, you are just not ready to succeed at scale.

It's more comfortable to tell ourselves that we are genuinely great, and we should have won. It's more rewarding to listen, learn, and keep improving our approach each and every time.

It's your choice. It just requires candor and a spirit that you will get there!

CHAPTER 7

THE RELEVANT LEADER

"A leader takes people where they want to go. A great leader takes people where they don't necessarily want to go, but ought to be."

—*Rosalynn Carter*

When we were clients, we met with countless agencies around the world.

We always found it perplexing why and when the top leaders would show up.

It seemed to be for a major pitch or just to "check in." Neither was what we were looking for.

Our view is that the most senior leaders of a firm should be there due to their vast experience and expertise. We wanted to tap into it!

Fast forward to today, and here is the advice we say aloud to ourselves to remind us of why any of us are relevant (or not) in a given setting.

Here are four key reminders for us to think through together. Imagine this as an informal note to CEOs of agencies from clients around the world.

#1—Talk about us, not you. When you walk in the room, we are not hoping you will regale us with the breadth of your offering, the number of offices you now have, or how many awards you just won at the latest industry-award function.

There is a reason we don't care. It's because we are thinking about why our stock price is more volatile today or how we will effectively reach one hundred thousand employees with a new set of corporate messages or whether or not our new product will launch successfully across thirty countries in its first year.

We don't have time or interest to hear about every single thing you do.

We have a lot of time for a discussion that is relevant to us. Help us advance our initiatives. And then we are good. We do care about an offering, an office, or an award if we can imagine the impact it could have on us. That's different.

Figure out what we care about. Understand our issues. Listen to us. Then you'll know what to talk about.

Your title is not relevant. Your insights and ideas are and will always be welcome.

#2 – Don't be a human survey. We can picture the extremely well-dressed executives who walk into our office or conference room. We can tell they haven't prepped. They aren't totally sure who we are or what we stand for. But they are senior people, so they will ask us questions to find out "how we are doing."

The only problem is we tell the truth to those we know and trust. If you are a senior leader and are not part of the daily team, your job is to be relevant and build trust. You are not a human survey machine.

We care about our agency team. We want them to succeed, and we need to know you care as much as we do about our team. Once we do, we're cool.

When you are interested in just striking up a conversation, we recommend reflecting on what you can do to help us, since your network and knowledge can often be valuable. Be useful *beyond the assignment.* When you are and we can trust you, you will know how your team is doing because we will proactively tell you.

#3 – Don't come in unprepared. Imagine this scenario. A final pitch is about to occur for what will be one of the world's top cancer drugs. The final agencies are coming in to pitch. The day before, the main competitor was approved with major press and momentum.

As one of the agencies was setting up to present, we asked them if they would not present right away and instead take a moment to reflect on yesterday's news and share with us what it means and how it might change their outlook for our cancer therapy. It was a softball question meant to give them a chance to show how smart and prepared they were.

The leader of the team babbled something about our drug. We repeated the question, and they all looked at each other in a panic. No one had paid attention to the news! And no one had a point of view!

The pitch was now over, but to be polite, we let them present and asked questions. We were nice hosts. That agency, by the way, never received any additional opportunities to present to our company.

Being prepared means you understand how the company works, you have checked the stock market, you know who their competitors are, and you know of any big moves we may have just made.

You are ready to hold a meaningful conversation with us that is aligned with our current needs.

If you are not prepared, just stay home. Always walk in ready to go far deeper than the meeting has time for.

#4 – Think long term in the short term. We are thinking about our careers, how we can build our network, and how we can strengthen our campaigns. We are not wondering if an agency will meet its organic growth target for the year.

If you help us succeed, we will be looking for many ways to expand what we do together. You may never have to ask since we know where to place our bets.

Help us make that decision easy.

In summary, if senior leaders use common sense and invest their time in us, it's easy to build a great future together. Yet, for some reason, this approach is a differentiator, rather than the norm. Not doing this is a form of intellectual laziness that the best firms will simply not tolerate.

The flip side is learning about the business of our clients is exciting, inspiring, and offers challenges that, quite frankly, drive us like nothing else. Embrace the work and the rest is easy.

LEADERSHIP INSIGHT

What Great Client Service Looks Like

I was at Dell, and our company was starting to build what would become a major and highly successful partnership with Salesforce.com. But in the beginning, like many relationships, we had our bugs. Both sides to be candid.

We hit one of these stumbling blocks, and we all got a bit heated during the workday. All of us just wanted to succeed, but we weren't quite seeing eye to eye on our next steps. The actual example isn't relevant. What happened next is.

I received a phone call around nine in the evening with an international ring. It was Marc Benioff, founder and CEO of Salesforce.com, calling me to understand what issues we were dealing with, how we could potentially resolve them, and what the best next steps could be.

He was calm, thoughtful, and focused.

As he was speaking, I realized that Marc was calling me from Switzerland, and it was three in the morning.

We figured it all out and were back on the path to building our partnership.

What I learned is that great client service often makes the most impact when you realize how much your partner cares about the relationship. This can occur in many different ways and doesn't mean you should fly to Switzerland to call everyone at three in the morning! But it does mean that you care as much as your client about the business you share, and it shows. You can't fake it. It's just who you are.

CHAPTER 8

CAN I BUILD A PRACTICE?

"You don't build a business.
You build people, and people build the business."
—*Zig Ziglar*

Your career is going well. Clients love you. Your team is responsive and enjoys their work. You have been involved in new business with some success. You are starting to develop a passion for key areas. And then you are asked, "Have you ever thought of building a practice?"

It's a question that is both exciting and a bit intimidating. We think, "Can I build a practice? Who would care if I did?" Our minds race.

Been there.

From both building practices and helping many leaders start or accelerate practices, we have all learned a few things along the way.

The building of a practice can be placed into a model that will provide instruction to you, whether you are twenty-two or fifty-two.

Here are the components of success:

#1—Desire to be the best—Great athletes train every day, so they are ready when their moment arrives. Great practice leaders ensure their offering is the best, their slides are excellent, and their story is tight. They work as long as they need to work. They prepare to "win" every time they pitch to a new client or present to a current client. They are not afraid to acknowledge they are here to build the best practice they are capable of building. You feel it.

#2 – Relevant expertise – Combination of book smart and street smart. You are viewed as being smart in your area and are known for being crafty. You have the ability to listen to a client and figure out what they need, whether it was directly said or not. Clients want to brainstorm with you.

#3 – Networks that generate leads – People like and respect you. Clients want to collaborate with you. People want to join your team. This leads to a never-ending pipeline for both. Great networks are the direct result of countless breakfast meetings, drinks after work, weekend phone calls, and just doing magnificent work for each and every client, since your clients will move on to their next opportunity and bring you along.

#4 – Ability to build a team – You are confident enough to hire at least four people smarter and better than you are (+4), so you can scale. You now support them to drive their success. The rest happens naturally.

#5 – Financial acumen – You treat finance as an equal partner and learn from your finance partner how to forecast, do capacity analysis, understand your P&L, and start to make more informed decisions.

As you can see, it takes effort to be the best. Let's assume you read these five components and think, "Yep, that's me." Great, now do this exercise to see how you are doing today.

List the improvements you have made for your firm in the last year. Be specific.

Outline the top three ways you are improving your expertise right now. Current plan.

Build a spreadsheet and write in the people who would take your call and likely hire you. Build at least a top ten.

Write down either the people or the skills you need for your +4 (top four direct reports).

Think of the last time you asked your financial leader to explain a concept to you.

Most likely, you will come up short in some of these areas, even if you are a practice leader today.

If you are a practice leader, you know what to do.

If you are about to become one, you can see the game plan.

If this idea is in the future, start working now so you ease into the role.

The best way to think of how you become a great practice leader is to realize it's not like being anointed by a king or queen. It's actually a reflection of how hard you have worked every day of your career to get ready for this exact moment.

The Roman philosopher Seneca once said, "Luck is what happens when preparation meets opportunity." Create your own luck.

CHAPTER 9

COMPETITIVE SPIRIT—WHAT IS YOUR STORY?

"Practice like you've never won. Play like you've never lost."

—*Michael Jordan*

Michael Jordan said that being cut from the varsity basketball team in high school has been a driving force for him his entire life. Heck, he mentioned it prominently in his Hall of Fame speech.

At this point, I would say he has made his point.

However, what many of us don't know is he wasn't actually cut from the team. In fact, he tried out for the Laney High School (North Carolina) varsity team as a sophomore and was asked to play on the junior varsity, since he was only 5'10". They needed to take his buddy, Leroy Smith, who was 6'7". Later on, he did make the varsity basketball team in high school.

The point of sharing this correction has a purpose.

All of us experience slights or perceived slights in our lives. It's what we do about these slights that define us.

I think of a slight as being a moment when someone else doesn't believe in our abilities, but we do.

We know what we are capable of doing. And we will prove to the world we are right.

I'll share a few of mine for perspective. When I was asked to join a pharmaceutical company to lead product communications for North

America at the age of twenty-nine, the executive search firm lead said, "I don't believe you will be successful in this job." I was stunned.

Years later, I was asked to join GCI and work for Bob Feldman, where Bob asked me to start what is now known as GCI Health. It was my first time as an entrepreneur and as employee one in a firm, I didn't have any clients, or an offering, and I could see the smirks in meetings of colleagues who were wondering when I would fail.

When I look back, of course, I realize that maybe they weren't really smirking, but I felt like they were. I was conditioned at this point in my life to think that maybe someone was doubting me.

For me, personally, it goes back to where I grew up in Millburn/Short Hills, New Jersey. I like to say half of the town was well off and the other half consisted of the people who made the town work—the police, fire department, public works, teachers, and more. That was the part I grew up in.

So, I was conditioned from an early age to run into people who had lower expectations for me than I did for myself. And I realized early in my life through my parents and people I watched that my future was going to be defined by me, no one else.

What it translates into is a desire to work harder, practice more, learn more, prepare more, so when you do get a chance to shine, you haven't left anything behind.

When I first joined sales, I consumed dozens of books and continually listened to audiotapes on how to sell. When I joined pharma, I took home medical books to learn how the heart or the central nervous system worked. When I started managing people, I read every book I could on how to manage and then continually asked leaders what they did or just watched them in action.

What I realized is that if you practice like you've never won, you can play like you've never lost, just like Jordan said.

So, in an odd way, I am thankful for those who underestimated me. It's the best motivation I could have ever had.

Stuff happens in our lives. Slights will occur. It is what you choose to do with slights that define you.

So, let's bring it back home to you. What should you, as a leader or future leader, look for when building a great team and firm?

Jordan's quote speaks to what I have seen great leaders of all ages do.

They "practice" continually. They ask questions, read, get degrees at night, and go deeper on client business than their peers. They want to be "ready" every time. There is a hunger that you can see, but maybe not explain. They have something to prove.

And when they get in front of clients, they are ready due to their practice habits. Maybe not perfect (Who is?), but ready.

So, they play like they never lost. In fact, they are excited about these client interactions.

What else have I learned?

Simple. Don't look at titles or grade point averages or compensation and imagine how good someone could be. Don't ignore them but keep focused on the intangibles.

Look for people who are always practicing their craft. Here are some examples:

They are involved in supporting organizations outside of work.

They are avid readers or creators. It could be reading, but it might be artwork, math formulas, or expertise they honed in government or nonprofits.

They love talking about their client's business, and you can see they learn like it is their business.

They care, and they can't wait to dig in to figure out the next challenge.

Their ambition is one that is driven by great practice habits, since when they get to play, they want to be ready at all times. They are confident in themselves, but not overconfident in how they present themselves. They don't need to be since that drive gives them a sort of inner peace.

Hire people like that every time you see them, and you can teach them the rest.

CHAPTER 10

IMAGINE WHEN THE DUST SETTLES

"Long-range planning does not deal with
the future decisions, but with the
future of present decisions."

—Peter Drucker

A client calls with a sense of immediacy, and we soon realize we have an emergency situation.

We gather the team, listen to the intakes, and quickly decide our next steps to provide the right support. Bing. Bang. Zoom.

It is this exact moment that many of us experience. But for those of us who excel in a crisis situation, we all describe the same type of personality trait that guides us.

When others become anxious, we become the least emotional and most pragmatic people in the room.

It is this ability to slow things down that allows us to deal with future decisions in the present.

Here is an example from my life:

> In July 2006, I was working at Dell when I received an email about a laptop in Osaka, Japan, that caught on fire. I immediately sent it to Michael Dell, and we soon met in his office. Without knowing the full extent of the issue, we started planning for a future recall.

This is part one. It was an immediate decision to make a present decision with the future in mind. The test I remember is simple: "What will customers think about us one year from now based on our actions today?"

Part two tested our resolve.

There were at least fourteen manufacturers who were all sourcing the same lithium-ion batteries from Sony. Everyone either had or would have this same issue, but no one was interested in joining us for a recall. So, we were all alone.

We reached out to the Consumer Product Safety Commission of the US government to begin the process of an extensive recall. An amazing Dell team, led by Alex Gruzen, set in place a battery replacement plan, and our team created a special website and wrote blog posts to narrate our rollout along with a full communications plan.

We led the industry, took the hit on the negative publicity, and, just like we predicted, every other company eventually had to admit they had the same issue.

We were transparent with our customers and implemented the largest battery recall in the industry at that time.

One year later, we knew from direct feedback that our customers appreciated our willingness to lead the way, since it surely decreased the overall hazard across the industry. And it was the right thing to do.

No surprise, but it turns out that customers always appreciate it when you do the right thing, even if it doesn't feel wonderful in the moment. We were even publicly thanked by the Consumer Product Safety Commission.

The decision was easy because we were making a future decision in the present.

This mindset is a combination of thinking fast and acting slow. A critical skill set to have in a crisis.

Do we always think ahead one year and imagine what we will all respect when the dust settles?

Or do we overreact in the moment and not really know how it will play out?

Slow down, think forward, and always believe that if you make the right call, you are in good shape, even if it feels uncomfortable in the short term.

Sidenote

Great hitters in baseball often say the ball looks bigger in pressure situations. They are slowing down the moment, while the crowd is going crazy.

This is what makes a great hitter. They appear to have more time than others, but they don't—it's a mindset.

CHAPTER 11

HOW TO VISUALIZE THE FUTURE OF YOUR FUNCTION

INSIDE THE MIND OF THE CHIEF COMMUNICATIONS OFFICER (CCO)

"If you don't know where you are going,
you'll end up someplace else."

— *Yogi Berra*

We often talk about how we need to think like our client.

It's easy to say, hard to do.

I have found that if you write down your thoughts about a function, you quickly see what is common to leaders with similar responsibilities.

When I was asked to think through the future of the chief communications officer's role, I wrote it from their perspective, which helps me informally test if the idea is worth including. It's a great exercise. Imagine doing so for any key position that is important to many of your client relationships. By the way, I believe clients should do the same related to agency partners.

Here is the review. It is simply one type of angle. You could write a series of posts like this based on how you want to view the CCO. In this case, I am thinking of their most common headaches.

The CCO's responsibilities involve how to understand, protect, and promote all aspects of a company, which is why we are the center point for leaders to reach.

Those of us who have been CCOs view our job as including the following:

We are responsible for the entire narrative of the company. We achieve this goal by focusing on the strategic messaging of the company and its divisions, external and internal, the spokespeople we allow to speak publicly, and the decisions made related to where/when/how we tell our story.

We serve the C-suite to ensure the voice of the CEO and the greater leadership team is effective in how they reach all audiences.

We are continually protecting the brand reputation of the company via issues management techniques that are often never known to the public.

We are zealots in ensuring that what we say publicly matches what we tell Main Street and Wall Street.

In the midst of all this, we may have a team launching a new product, while another is developing an internal communications plan for manufacturing, while reporters are digging into an issue, and we are ensuring the CEO's next speech is A+. As an example, when I was at Novartis, I had a team of 340 people across the globe, so the job never ended as I responded to team members across time zones from Japan to Jersey.

So, what's inside the mind of a CCO when we're talking with them? Here's what I remember and continue to see in colleagues to this day:

How will we ensure that our messaging is current across the world? I don't have time to approve everything, nor does my team, but I want a system that can aid us in keeping messaging on track and telling us when it is off track.

How do we ensure content is approved and truly ready to be shared?

How do we age out content once it is no longer current/viable?

How do I quickly create the content I need in a crisis/issue?

I have Q&As for every issue you can imagine. How could I more effectively prepare our messages for issues, so we can go from Q&A writing to a more agile system?

How do we create more content and not break the bank?

When is someone going to build an image/video/content library for CCOs? We're tired of hearing about the next DAM for marketing.

Do we have all these speeches and other collateral we create for events? How could we leverage key content? No one has time to do this, so it never happens. What a waste.

How can I get my shared media team to have agile content to share on social channels, so one person can scale their efforts across the globe?

How could I have this same effort during a crisis, so we are the most proactive company when we want to be?

Will our approval system work well in getting content approved for your system? And what happens to content approval if we are recreating new agile content? Is the intent the same? How can we prove it?

Is there a system that can show what we put out internally and externally that can match up versus our strategic goals and messages and tell us where we need to place more effort and why?

That's a start on what is inside the mind of a CCO. Now, let's also discuss their initial view of any new platform they are asked to review. Our minds think like this:

Why do I need to see this new platform? A team member becomes intrigued and comes to see me as I am thinking about five things at once. My response? Headline it. What does it do? Why do we care? That's what I would ask our team. Tell me why, and if not super clear, pass. Why pass? Because we have a few vendors per day trying to break in. We know most of them waste our time, and our time is our most precious asset.

When we meet, we want to hear how we can get our problems solved. Other than basic pleasantries, we don't want to hear a long story about your firm. We just don't have time, and to be candid, we don't care, at least right now. We would prefer to get right into what you do and how it helps us. We'll learn more about you as time goes on. If we are future partners, we have plenty of time to bond.

When we listen to solutions, if we don't hear answers to our problems, we know you don't know our world, so we start tuning out. We remain polite, but nothing happens in follow-up.

If you come in through someone higher up the food chain, we are wary. Now, it may be political (or not), depending on who it came in from. Nothing good or bad, just reality, so we are more careful.

We are looking at the platform and team and wondering, "Will these folks make our life simpler, or are they just selling and running?"

We think of pilots, partly to get our own team to buy in, since they are burned out on solutions that rarely work. Heck, Microsoft leads in that category, as good as they are overall.

But if we can see you understand us and can solve our problems and exist to make our lives simpler, then we are going to go as fast as you can handle. I can think of examples where I have stopped a conversation and said, "I'll give you $500k to get started. Let's go talk about how to get moving." The funny thing is the new partner still wants to sell, so you have to say, "I get it, don't need more, let's get going." And you go from there.

The good news for enlightened companies is that most software firms that try to sell into companies are thinking about their amazing story, their amazing platform, and their amazing people and why they are going to have an amazing IPO someday. The client is thinking the opposite—how do you improve our story? Will this platform scale and make our lives easier? Will your people ensure our people succeed? Will this be more cost-effective for us in the long term?

It's cognitive dissonance when the two sides don't get each other. When they do, the magic of a strong relationship leads to outcomes that make us all smile.

Take a function you care deeply about and write out their perspective. It helps you go deeper in your understanding of the clients you serve or the client you are hoping to be.

LEADERSHIP INSIGHT

Be Respectful to Everyone

When my grandfather, Leo Didur, arrived in the US from Ukraine many years ago, the kids threw stones at him and called him names because he spoke Russian. He became a hotel doorman, then a bartender, and eventually, he bought a bar. He named it Leo's Tavern.

Leo Didur looked past the slights and pursued his American dream.

My parents always taught us that we are all equal, and you show it by showing compassion for everyone. You play with the kid who no one wants to play with. You help out the person everyone forgot.

We followed those simple guidelines and still do.

When we work in firms and are celebrated for our success, why does that give us the right to be different?

It doesn't.

You have an opportunity every day to pay it forward by just being normal to everyone you encounter. Make time to get to know the new team member who may be more introverted. Help a person struggling who may just need more advice from you.

Remember, we are all the same.

CHAPTER 12

CELEBRATE AND LEARN FROM YOUR MISTAKES

"If you tell the truth, you don't have to remember anything."

—*Mark Twain*

I remember hurriedly walking past rows and rows of cubes in Dell's headquarters to have an update meeting for a new project. Someone stopped me and asked why something didn't happen on time. I started to explain why we didn't get there.

The leader interrupted me and said, "We don't tell stories here. Explain why it didn't work, and then tell us what you will do to make it happen. And then move forward."

It was a moment of validation and freedom that I have never forgotten. One that became branded in my brain that we can learn as much from failure as we do from success.

My career has been spent mainly in the world of life sciences and technology.

Both industries learn by iteration. Most efforts fail, but they learn from each failure as they search for a new treatment or develop a new platform. In fact, without a string of failures, they would never figure out the solution in nearly every case.

If scientists and technologists made excuses, they would go out of business!

It really made me think about why we rationalize our failures rather than celebrate them in our industry.

We know this behavior of learning is critical in the lab. So, why does it change in the office?

Yes, I know. Most cultures say they reward honesty, but in reality, they reward honesty most of the time, as long as it is not too direct and everyone still feels good.

This leads to a culture that, quite frankly, starts to avoid learning from its mistakes.

> *We become storytellers. We always have a reason why something didn't work.*
>
> *We become rationalizers. We didn't like that client anyway.*
>
> *We become enablers. You did a wonderful job, even though we really thought the work was mediocre.*

What's missing is simple.

Direct feedback. Direct accountability. Direct next steps.

The good news is that being direct and being responsible for all our actions is more rewarding and more fun, when done in a non-emotional manner.

If we embrace failure and see it as an opportunity to gain experience, we improve each time. A fitting example occurs when we "almost" win a new business pitch. Do we dissect what worked, and are we completely candid about what didn't work? If we are, our win rates go up over time. If not, we hover in the same area and repeat the same mistakes. But at least everyone is happy, right?

If we take the time to figure out how to align with each client, we realize that sometimes we don't have the right team to match up with our client. Or we may be doing the work, but not any extras that surprise and delight. We start to see how we can improve versus how the client can improve. This is important since we only control one side of this conversation.

We welcome criticism of our work. We realize that great writers are born after years of critical feedback from their editors. The best creatives have had their work torn apart by their peers, and they learn how to improve each time. Now let's imagine you are a professional baseball player, and you are at practice. Does your coach tell you how wonderful you are and shower you with praise, or does your coach tell you to move your elbow up to improve your swing, follow through when you throw the ball, or ask you why you took a third strike?

Great coaches watch what you do and show you how to improve. They tell it like it is, and we accept it, since we know our coach wants the same thing we do—to be successful and win.

This is why great cultures celebrate and learn from their mistakes.

Everyone wants to learn how to improve. Imagine a world more like this.

Managers are direct in their feedback. Teams are direct in figuring out what to do next and having collegial discussions with their managers on how to make it happen.

New business leaders publish the two to three key learnings from each pitch, showing what we can do to improve next time.

Client reviews include a section on how our team can improve its habits and results.

When someone starts to tell a story, we ask them to stop and focus on what the key learning is and what we can do to improve. Each and every time.

It can all be done without extra emotion since we are trying to accomplish the same objective—how to become the best in each situation.

If we realize that an inability to address the truth actually devalues our firm and our ability to serve our clients, we embrace the need to change.

How can you tell that this approach is part of your culture? It's easy.

You welcome input. You listen to how to improve, and you do it non-emotionally, since your common goal is to improve. You also listen more closely to the conversations you are having in your firm.

Do you hear the excuses and the stories more clearly now?

You probably have work to do. That's normal.

In a take-off of Mark Twain's quote, if you tell the truth and ask the same of your team, you will all know exactly what to do next to improve.

CHAPTER 13

PURPOSE STARTS WITH EACH OF US

"Alone we can do so little; together we can do so much."

—*Helen Keller*

This is the importance of our workplaces.

If we are all working hard as individuals, we'll never fully unlock new ideas or optimize how we learn from each other.

The best organizations are filled with teams who have decided that their mission and vision are their North Star. It drives their decision-making every day.

Excellence in the workplace always sounds so easy, yet it is one of the more vexing situations that every C-suite leader thinks about.

It is our view that the details matter and every program that touches an employee is worthy of the excellence we all deserve. It's why, over the years, our range of work includes employee-sponsored healthcare, voluntary benefits, retirement benefits, workplace well-being and mental health, recruiting, benefits brokers, HR technology, benefits delivery, and workplace consulting.

The workplace is more than a message. It reflects the actions we take across the board to make our business life seamless, supportive, and sensible. It is within this framework that our larger story can be heard.

As you may be able to tell, we are passionate about the workplace, which is why we always love collaborating with leaders who have the desire to evolve it.

Our offering is designed to provide insights, develop actionable campaigns, and stay focused on making a difference that is long lasting. You might say sustainable.

It's why we say that "purpose" starts with each of us.

Many companies today talk about finding their purpose.

The answer is inside each of us.

Sometimes that North Star needs some sharpening. Other times it needs to be created.

But the journey starts with each of us. And from there, we decide to make a difference in how we work together.

CHAPTER 14

SUCCESSION PLANNING—WHAT DO I DO?

"One of the things we often miss in succession planning is that it should be gradual and thoughtful, with lots of sharing of information and knowledge and perspective, so that it's almost a non-event when it happens."

—*Anne M. Mulcahy*

You can't say it better than Anne Mulcahy.

The big question is, why do we miss so often in succession planning?

I have an idea from watching leaders for many years. Here are my top five:

#1—The founder avoids the topic. Many people who start companies secretly wonder if they can ever do it again. They are thrilled to be leading the way and don't let themselves think about an exit. They might be reserving the firm for their own children (a great way to avoid the conversation), or they just make it a topic that can never be discussed (I'll never leave, why did you bring this up?).

#2—The company lacks a +4 organizational model. Great leaders are continually looking to find four leaders who are as good or better than they are to report to them and then, in turn, do the same. If you are always focused on building your best four reports and your reports do the same, then you create a very, very strong team.

#3 – Love of money leads to procrastination. The founder is enjoying the money and plans to think of succession next year. And the following year. They'll get to that succession stuff, eventually. Probably hire some expert to tell them what to do. Sort of like their commitment to update their will and estate someday. "Someday" takes too long to happen.

#4 – An inability to realize every leader has an expiration date. Some founders have trouble believing that anyone could be smarter and better than they are. Kind of odd when you think about it. PWC did a study of 2,500 public companies that found the median tenure of a CEO is five years and only 19 percent stayed more than ten years. Yet founders often stay far longer. Smart? Or do founders tend to stay on too long?

#5 – The realization that you are *always* succession planning. If you treat every hire as important and imagine your most junior hire having the potential to grow into a future president, then you have the right mentality. Succession planning will take care of itself in this manner. But if you look at new hires as people to do work, so you can stay on longer as the founder, it's not the same.

The most important point of succession planning is also the scariest for many people.

You should always be planning your obsolescence and then be thrilled when it happens.

What a great achievement to leave an organization and it continues to do well, perhaps even better!

If the organization will do worse when you leave, then you really messed up.

Start thinking about succession planning now and never stop thinking about it. And if you don't own a firm or lead a function, remember that you should think the same way. Your day will arrive if you stay focused and keep creating value and knowledge that makes it possible for you to lead the way.

I'll leave you with one other thought.

The word succession incorporates "success" in it.

Doing it well means we are planning for success for everyone in the organization over time.

It should be fun, meaningful, and rewarding, over time. In fact, it should be a non-event, just like Ms. Mulcahy said.

CHAPTER 15

A MOM'S ADVICE—PERSPECTIVE FOR OUR CAREERS

"The only person you are destined to become
is the person you decide to be."
—*attributed to Ralph Waldo Emerson*

When I was a little kid growing up in Millburn, New Jersey, we had a blast.

Most of the time we would run out the door to play sports, ride our bikes for miles, go hiking in the woods, or just play step ball at our school, hoping the ball would clear the third highest electrical wire and be declared a home run. We would continue until our parents hit the bell for dinner on our front porch or the streetlights went off, whichever came first. Then, we hightailed it home.

Every now and then, life wasn't so perfect. We had a few bullies. We had some kids who got picked on who didn't deserve it. Not everything was roses in every home when the doors closed. We had the issues all neighborhoods have.

I would talk about these things with my mom, and she would share her philosophy on life to guide my thinking. And it led us to think a bit differently.

My brother, sister, and I were kids who would call up a kid getting picked on and ask if we could play with them. We would make sure we looked after someone at school who might need a friend. We would defend someone who was getting bullied. We tried to do the right things, and this was reinforced at home. We were on a quiet mission to do the right thing. But we still asked questions.

My mom is one of the better philosophers I've ever met, and one of her thoughts is worth sharing, since it has been a guide for my entire career.

She would say, "Bobby, always imagine you are at the end of your life, and you are looking backward. Ask yourself if you have lived your best life. Are you proud of how you have handled each day and each decision?"

That's heavy advice for a kid who probably had chocolate stains on his shirt and needed a haircut, but it was powerful, and it stuck with me.

Most great advice is simple and profound.

Many years later, I think of this advice at least once per week.

It makes me grimace sometimes, since I know I didn't handle things as well as I could have. Most of the time, it serves as a reinforcement that it's worth going the extra mile to do the right thing, whether or not the other person will ever acknowledge it. That part doesn't really matter. What matters is doing the right thing.

I've been surprised at where this advice has led me.

If I look back, I've never hesitated to donate my time to a nonprofit focused on improving society in some manner. I've never hesitated to support our country via teaching and consulting. This can lead to many long evenings and weekends of giving time to a greater cause. And I'm always glad I did it.

In day-to-day work, it causes me to look at the entire firm we lead with the same eye.

"Will everyone in this firm look back someday and see their time together as one of the most productive and valuable times in their career?"

This is where personal and leadership advice merge.

As leaders, we need to imagine the future every day for our clients. We need to do the same for the people we lead.

Are we doing our best every time to provide the most value to our clients?

What are we doing to improve our firm, so others benefit?

Are we reaching out to a peer in our firm who might benefit from time together?

Are we doing what is inconvenient but important to make a difference?

I end with another simple observation.

We will never be perfect or do all the right things. Life isn't that easy.

But we can look back someday with pride that we did all we were capable of doing.

And that is worth thinking about.

Thanks Mom.

LEADERSHIP INSIGHT

Don't Chase the Trends to Be Popular— Just Be a Great Leader

We all know the firms that try to offer every perk they can imagine, so they are viewed as being hip and with it.

Five years later, can you remember any of those firms?

You can't, and neither can their employees.

What we remember are great leaders who help accelerate our career growth, give us new opportunities to explore, and really care about our life journey.

Five years later, can you remember these firms and their leaders?

Yes! They become part of your life story.

Great leaders will be your partners and mentors forever. Those who shower you with perks are probably more scared that you will leave than focused on your future.

Choose leaders who will help you build your future, and you will have chosen well.

CHAPTER 16

THE MAGIC OF A MOMENT

"Nothing is black or white, nothing's 'us or them.'
But then there are magical, beautiful things in the world.
There are incredible acts of kindness and bravery,
and in the most unlikely places, and it gives you hope."

—*Dave Matthews*

At the age of seven, the big kids asked me to play baseball at Slayton Field in Millburn, New Jersey. This was like getting asked to play in the pros at that age, since the rest of the kids were anywhere from eight to twelve years old.

So here I was, seven years old and, in my mind, on the fast track to becoming the shortstop for the New York Yankees, a team my dad had played for (Triple-A).

Meanwhile, I was still using an old glove of my dad's that was past its prime. So, I started a campaign to get a new glove. Why not!

A few weeks later, we walked into Masco's, a sports warehouse in Summit, New Jersey, to look at gloves, and sure enough, I found the perfect one for me. As we walked towards the cash register, my dad asked the owner to talk on the side. I remember he was both happy for me and a bit anxious, which I could not figure out.

Years later, it struck me that my dad had figured out a payment plan or a special deal with the owner, since it was stretching our bank account to get me a glove. But darned if I wasn't going to get one!

This piece of cowhide was the most important object on earth for me. I broke in the glove with string and oils. I played catch with my brother constantly and did everything possible to make that glove my own.

I could definitely field ground balls better, and I was off to what would be a fun "career" in baseball.

Over time, it started to sink in that this glove was also quite special for my dad. He could have said no or delayed the purchase, but he didn't, and his joy was equal to mine. Getting a glove for his son was as magical a moment for him as it was for me.

In the professional world, we all play a role in creating magical moments that we don't realize are happening. It can be from an act of kindness, taking time to meet with someone who didn't expect we would make time, or just making a phone call during the day.

After 35+ years in our business, I have been repeatedly surprised to run into colleagues I worked with in the past and hear things like:

"I remember when you told me XYZ, and it changed my career"; or "I'll never forget you wrote me a letter of recommendation for business school"; or "Remember when you stood up in front of us and said ABC."

Magical moments are not planned. They occur because we care about everyone we interact with. These moments are unscripted, and often the interaction itself seems normal.

We can't always buy a baseball glove for a seven-year-old. But we can make the extra call at the end of the day when we are bone tired. We can hear in the voice of a friend that they need to talk and take them out to breakfast. We can support a friend even when it is inconvenient to us in that particular moment.

We create many of these moments without knowing it. And that's the way it's supposed to be.

Those you impact remember forever. Over time, you'll see the benefits in ways you would never expect.

CHAPTER 17

THE MYTH OF "GUT FEEL"

WHAT GREAT COUNSELORS HAVE IN COMMON

"Intuition is a very powerful thing, more powerful than intellect."

—*Steve Jobs*

You have surely heard someone say, "Wow, Peter Drucker has an amazing gut feel. I don't know how he always figures out the right thing to do."

We do know the answer if we think about it.

Leaders with a great "gut feel" or "intuition" usually have this going on. People that we look up to for their ability to think ahead often spend their time reading on airplanes, catch up on more reading on the weekends, and constantly push themselves to understand what is happening in their world. It is no accident.

Relentless reading to learn more on a wide variety of topics—*Peter Drucker believed that we learn best when we read about economics, psychology, social science, history, ethics, and more. It is that ongoing desire to learn widely and not get stuck in an echo chamber that separates us.*

Experience that leads to strong pattern recognition—*Humans and the organizations they run continually run into the same issues faced many times before. Great counselors have an ability to store this information in their memory, which helps them see a new pattern earlier than most. We refer to it sometimes as "I know how the movie ends." We can also see when a new pattern, one we may not be familiar with, is* *emerging. The ability to not immediately lock in is what separates the good from the great.*

Let us take a moment here to imagine super talented people who are not counselors yet display this behavior in ways that blow our mind.

We heard Beck play recently in Austin, and he had a steel guitar player he met at 2:00 a.m. the night before in a bar on stage. The guitarist accompanied Beck for two and a half hours the next day in front of 2,500 people and played flawlessly, playing songs he had not played with Beck before.

The best traders on Wall Street are making 50x the number of decisions of their peers. This massive difference in experience helps separate them from the pack. Their pattern recognition is off the charts.

The most prolific movie directors have an uncanny ability to figure out what we will love repeatedly. They are students of the audience they serve.

So, it is not intelligence; its intuition built over time that separates us. Sure, it is good to be smart, but graduating from a great school and being book smart is different from being street smart. And great counselors are of the streets.

It is a form of subconscious learning. Facts and experiences stored in the back of your mind guide decisions you are making in real time. We have heard leaders say they can "smell it," whether it is an opportunity or how to deal with an issue. They just know.

You might be reading this and thinking, "Great, I don't have all this experience. What do I do?"

Well, the answer is the same for all of us.

- Read widely in a range of topics, including areas you don't normally explore. The liberal arts approach to life is a good one. Read fiction and nonfiction.
- Practice constantly. Immerse yourself in issues and opportunities continually and regularly listen for feedback on what worked and what did not, so your brain can subconsciously store this knowledge for future use.

- Try new models. Learn new techniques. Think about what is next every day, not just now and then.
- Watch the people you believe have a great gut feeling and ask them how they do it. They will not explain it all that well, but they will give you tips on how they practice, read, and prepare.
- Be an intellectual explorer.

Great counselors are built over time. They are some of the most well-read and deeply informed people you will ever meet.

You can be one if you put in the time.

CHAPTER 18

THE TOXIC LEADER—WHY WE SHARE THEM WITH COMPETITORS

"The final relationship that cannot be ignored is with disrupters: They are individuals who cause trouble for sport—inciting opposition to management for a variety of reasons, most of them petty. Usually these people have good performance—that's their cover—and so they are endured or appeased. A company that manages people well takes disrupters head-on. First, they give them very tough evaluations, naming their bad behavior and demanding it change. Usually, it won't. Disrupters are a personality type. If that's the case, get them out of the way of people trying to do their jobs. They're poison."

—*Jack Welch*

The toughest management decision is often the easiest once we think about it for a minute.

When a baseball team wins the World Series or a basketball team comes out of nowhere to win the NCAA tournament, we ask why the team was so successful. We are told the team has built a unique "chemistry" that they can't quite explain.

In reality, they can explain it, and I will share why.

We all want individuals and leaders who think team-first. Teammates who wake up and think about how they can provide value to anyone they interact with, regardless of any credit they may deserve or receive.

This selfless approach helps us all reach our best selves. We feel like we are unlocking our potential. It's fun and inspiring to work with teammates who think like this.

Toxic leaders do not think like this.

The problem is, it is often difficult to spot them at first. That is, of course, different if you have been watching them for decades.

Here is how you can tell you have an issue:

They are definitely talented, but also often quite smart, overconfident, and self-centered. In the agency world, they are the leaders who say, "Well, you know, this client will only work with me. That is why we have this business." Or you give them your work, and they say, "This is crap. I'll have to fix it."

They cannot be bothered teaching their teammates how to build a relationship with a client who likes them or to show someone how they can do better next time. Why? Well, it is part of the power they generate for themselves.

Toxic leaders know how to talk the right game in public but act different in private.

They often build a 1:1 relationship with a senior leader, where they can ask for special compensation, trash someone, or otherwise look for ways to manipulate the system. A toxic leader will focus on manipulating one person at a time, since they know they have near zero chance of influencing the larger leadership team. It's one of the reasons we have always advocated that there should never be any light between leaders in a firm.

They can manipulate a person. They are far less successful trying to change a leadership group.

They are very eager to team up and build business together. Except, when you look at their track record, you have trouble identifying whose career they nurtured. They will support promotions of team members like everyone else, but they are not thinking of how to unlock a person's full value.

When you think about their track record, you realize that either no one or nearly no one is ever recruited directly by this person to join the firm. Reason? Simple. Those who worked with them in the past do not want to do it again.

They are often more argumentative with other leaders.

They develop their own systems of work that others cannot quite figure out.

They bad mouth their peers with senior leadership at opportune moments.

Anything bad that happens to them just reinforces their victim status. After all, they are the best in the industry and others are preventing them from getting to where they need to be.

Toxic leaders are tiring. They are smart in how they create the image in our brains that they are indispensable. They wear out those they report to, while great leaders are inspiring to meet and talk with and think about how to tackle problems together. We cherish our time together!

Toxic leaders are productive.

When we stop for a minute, we see their trail and realize they do not fit, but we sometimes hesitate because they are good at a few things. They try to convince us the relationships they build are solely dependent on their genius. They are smart in how they build their protections.

Now, if we take a minute and go back to winning teams, when you look closer at their chemistry, you hear things like this:

- We police ourselves. We do not let teammates get out of hand.
- We park our egos at the door. No one is better than the next person.
- We run through walls for our teammates. No question.

And when asked who won a game, each leader points to the other leaders who made it possible. They would rather walk away than take credit.

The subtleties of an effective team are actually clear when we know what to look for.

Now, can anyone have a dreadful day or moment? Of course. Just because someone says something wrong or does something that isn't smart, doesn't mean they are toxic. But over time, if you see a pattern, you know the answer.

You have the equivalent of a corporate virus. And it is best to deal with it as soon as you can.

In our experience, every time a toxic leader was removed, those who interacted with them quietly felt relieved. We cannot think of a time where they missed the person.

Our goal is to never let toxic leaders in the door, but if they do sneak in, we will find them and "share them with competitors."

FIRM GROWTH

CHAPTER 19

HOW TO SELL IN A PILOT—THE RULE OF THREE

"If opportunity doesn't knock, build a door."

—Milton Berle

We have a great new idea. We have spent countless hours getting it ready to share with our clients. We know this is a big deal.

But no one is calling us up and asking for it.

That's not the best way to do things. It often results in us building the solution no one asked for.

Instead, we use what we call the "rule of three."

When we are with clients, we make time to describe new ideas. When we have at least three clients say some version of, "That's a great idea. I want that," then we know we are ready to build.

The next phase is the pilot itself.

Clients who take the chance to pilot should get unique deals.

Make it inexpensive, often in the $25k to $75k range.

Make it relatively quick to see results. Think two to three months.

Only do a few pilots until you work the kinks out.

As the pilot turns into a product, make sure your thought leadership about your innovation includes the client leaders who took a chance with you. Ensure they get full credit.

Now, how do we get to the ideas that lead to the rule-of-three pilot?

We map out the unmet needs for our clients. Literally write them down on a piece of paper. We whiteboard how to solve them. We try to write up solutions. We visualize what they can look like.

It is often frustrating. We can't quite get there. But we keep trying because we know the unmet need is noticeably clear.

I have found that leaving half-baked solutions on a special whiteboard for weeks or months and letting people add to it can spark new ideas. Sometimes we temporarily give up, clear our heads, and come back refreshed.

One hundred percent of the time, the ideas are based on unmet needs. Zero percent of the time are they based on someone's untested idea.

Build excellence in dissecting the problem, and you will become strong in creating solutions.

Be fair in how you pilot and share credit widely.

And never forget the rule of three.

LEADERSHIP INSIGHT

What Efforts Do You Make to Improve That Are Uncomfortable?

I remember taking a Saturday class for my MBA, then spending Sunday doing work for my job and studying for class and just feeling exhausted. Sort of a love/hate relationship. It is not easy.

Many of us work with military veterans. Imagine their days defending our country. Not nearly as easy as being stuck in a commute to an air-conditioned office.

- How often do you do something that is hard?
- Do you support nonprofits and dedicate time at night or on weekends to share your skills?
- Do you stay up late to work on new ideas?
- How often do you read to learn?
- What does a long day of work look like for you?

If your life is always comfortable and predictable, you probably aren't pushing yourself as much as you could. If that is a choice, all good. If you want to lead a firm or a major team someday, well, get moving. It doesn't just get handed to you.

Make efforts to improve yourself that are sometimes uncomfortable.

As they say, no pain, no gain.

CHAPTER 20

METRICS SERVE AS THE NARRATOR OF OUR STORIES

"The problem with internet quotes is that you can't always depend on their accuracy."

—Abraham Lincoln, 1864 (not confirmed)

We all agree most dashboards are a waste of time. We love poking fun at their creation and lament at the time wasted in building one after another for those who want to know the "results."

That is our mistake. Leaders do not want to know the results. They want to know the story and, more importantly, what they need to keep doing, stop doing, or start doing.

We call them actionable insights. When we hear a great insight, we know what we need to do next. The data is speaking to us.

Stop for a moment and imagine you are going out for a jog right now. As you walk out the door and loosen up, you turn on a podcast from work that you need to hear to catch up. It starts with, "Our new car's campaign led to 54,212 people viewing our site; 27,235 people are from California, and 37 percent subscribed to our email."

You cannot switch off that podcast fast enough. Borrrrring.

Instead, imagine if you turned it on and heard, "Most auto critics predicted that our new electric car, Lightning, would never get out of the manufacturing plant. They just could not agree on when we would fail.

We remember when Emily, our CEO, said, 'Well, we can't wait for that first strike of lightning to wake up these critics, who are stuck in the past.' And sure enough, our very own bolt of innovation is resonating with our core audience. Our first-ever advertising campaign led to 54,212 people viewing our site in the first month, which was three times as many as we expected. More importantly, about half of them are from California, which is where we spent 90 percent of our campaign dollars, and one-third of those who heard about us signed up for more information. Our model is working, and your efforts are making a difference. People care."

It is a simple example because most of our insights at work are not as exciting as announcing the next music festival, yet we still want to be inspired. We want to understand the nuances and hope someone cares enough to narrate our business life.

What is missing in metrics is often narration. Together, the two tell the story, one filled with actionable insights that shape behavior.

Let us quickly break down what that means.

When we listen to our favorite podcast outside of work, we are guided through an experience. An inspiring presentation on YouTube walks us through a story with scenarios and anecdotes. We are listening to a story. We are paying attention.

Very few dashboards "make sense," and even fewer hold our attention. Here's part of what is missing:

We must engage the listener. We have short attention spans, but if we are hooked, we will take the time to listen. If we assume we have babble ahead of us, we tune out, daydreaming about what's for lunch.

To open the audience's mind, you must tell them something they didn't know. We call these actionable insights, since you listen, learn, and realize what you should do during the presentation.

If you get instructions on what to do next, pay attention. If you get justification for what you did in the past, fall into a hazy moment of polite non-listening. We do not want the person presenting to feel bad, so we just intellectually ignore them.

A narration of metrics is centered on the actions of our audience. It is incumbent on us to bring these characters and their stories to life to personalize our insights. It's why anecdotes aligned with insights can powerfully reinforce conclusions. Anecdotes untethered to results have the opposite effect. They are distracting.

Reflect on the last movie you enjoyed. While it played, you were in the moment. You were also on that trip to Mars or trying to catch the bad guy.

A great narration of our professional world transports us into the world of our customers or our employees. We feel like we are there. We feel in the moment as we talk about what is happening.

And that is quite different from staring at numbers that show "we improved 2.3 points in satisfaction from last quarter." I have never known what that means. If we said, "Our analytics are showing that three new drivers of behavior are impacting our audience, which are X, Y, and Z. We believe it is these factors, plus our new campaign that focuses on ABC, that have caused a temporary increase in satisfaction. What is interesting is that most of this improvement has occurred in women aged twenty-five to thirty-five who live in the Northeast, who love to compete in 10ks and live in large cities." You have me thinking, but I want more. I am listening.

When we are transported, we are more open minded. When we can understand how the metrics update ties into our overall story, we want to know more. And when we know we will hear how we can improve, we are waiting to learn more.

Metrics provide a chance to become the narrator in chief for a brand or an organization.

It is not easy, but it is a critical skill that will create an advantage in the market, since so few do it well.

If you care about shaping the thinking and actions of any organization, then you need to become an expert at understanding how to build the right metrics-driven presentations that narrate, inspire, warn, and clarify what is next for the leadership team.

Think of your mission as one where you represent the audience. It is your job to ensure their story is being heard, so the organization you represent can align the needs of both groups.

CHAPTER 21

ONE SLIDE, ONE PARAGRAPH, ONE PRICE

"Simplicity is the ultimate sophistication."

—*Leonardo da Vinci*

We live in our own heads. We spend our days thinking of great ideas. Fine tuning models. Figuring out complexities others haven't. And we come up with new ways to innovate.

Then we explain them. Oh boy....

We have twenty slides, we talk for twenty minutes, and we weave a story that ultimately makes sense, but the listener isn't sure what to do next.

We have just complicated our vision. We lose opportunities to bring on new clients. And yet they like us. They say we are smart. But they don't see a path forward right now.

Sound familiar?

If you have a great model, make it genuinely great by simplifying it.

A song lyric made famous by George Thorogood illustrates this point.

Thorogood took a blues song written by Rudy Toombs and played by Amos Milburn in 1953 and made it famous with his song, "One Bourbon, One Scotch, One Beer." What's interesting about this iconic tune is that this one sentence doesn't occur until the fifty-second line in the song!

He saw the brilliance of this one line and made it the title when it was re-released in 1977. It took twenty-four years to unlock the power of this one song.

In our world, it's a simple menu.

"One slide, one paragraph, one price." Admittedly, it is not an exciting lyric, and I would not expect Taylor Swift or Drake to make it famous someday. But it works in our world.

When you have a model that you believe is scalable and clients will benefit from, just follow this simple three-step approach:

- *Explain the model in one slide and give the model a name.* Brand it.
- *Describe it in one paragraph.* Make every word count.
- *Give it one price.* Let the price go up or down based on duration and scope.

And see what happens. If your model is valuable, you'll be pleasantly surprised at how well this works.

When our clients can quickly understand our models, they can explain them inside their companies, and the magic happens. Innovation occurs. And if you drink (I don't), you can sit back and enjoy a bourbon, scotch, or beer, although I do not recommend all three.

CHAPTER 22

HOW TO BUILD A THOUGHT LEADERSHIP PLAN

"The fundamental law of human beings is interdependence.
A person is a person through other persons."

—*Archbishop Desmond Tutu*

Imagine you are thinking about how to share how to develop a thought leadership plan for key clients with your team. You can hear it in the conference rooms of so many firms. "We need to do more thought leadership. Let's get something moving here."

We know we should do more, but we rarely plan it out, since we feel like we are busy and will "do it" as we have time. Well, that rarely works. Instead, here is an example of a more thoughtful approach.

DEVELOPING A THOUGHT LEADERSHIP PLAN

A strategic thought leadership plan will open the minds of our peers to further our discussion. This type of approach leads to "intellectual trust" and a belief that our firm will always be thinking about "what's next," which, of course, is a major part of our brand promise to the world.

Our plan will be centered on the premise that we must all challenge ourselves intellectually to think of what is truly "next" and how we can express our thinking. Whether the idea is small or large, it is always iterating the current truth of the marketplace.

Each leader will decide how they best express their thinking and follow this path. It can be via video, audio, writing, animation, or any other form of expression.

We will always look for ways to conduct thought leadership with current or future clients. Not all the time, since their internal regulations can limit what we say, but we will strive to conduct at least 50 percent of our work with peers to build stronger relationships and reach a wider audience.

The ways that we will create thought leadership will occur via the following areas, in most cases:

Blog posts – an easy way to express our thinking, post on LinkedIn, share in social channels, and see how our followers react.

Columns – a more formal way to position our thinking in a publication that adds credibility to our idea.

Podcasts – a great way to stretch our minds and discuss a range of thoughts with a particular theme.

Videos – if we show and tell, we will impact the audience versus just being a talking head. Visualize the concept and narrate its importance.

Panels – a terrific way to share ideas, similar to blog posts, and gauge interest.

Keynotes – the equivalent of a column. We are more formally taking a position.

Special events – we create events to leverage existing meetings, e.g., a special roundtable for marketers during CES in a side room, or we create our own events, e.g. the Storytizing Summit at SXSW, and invite clients to speak and join us in the audience.

Books – the most formal way of codifying a central theme of thinking we view as important to share.

Note: *The best thought leaders spend some of their time finding opportunities for current and future clients. Offering an opportunity for a column, a panel, or a keynote outside of any financial relationship is a wonderful way to show our respect for another leader.*

NEXT UP IS "WHAT DO I DO AS A LEADER?"

This addresses a simple question that most well-known thought leaders ask themselves: "What do I want to be known for in five to ten years, and why is that relevant to what I do?" Top thought leaders (think CEOs of the world) do not veer from this path. Michael Dell is known for his operational excellence. Steve Jobs left us wondering what was next. Ken Frazier showed us how a purposeful leader can manage a Fortune 500 company (Merck).

Think of what your brand is about. Write it down and say it aloud.

Now, let's pull this all together into a personal plan you can keep on a piece of paper or just do as part of your normal workflow.

#1 – What is my personal brand? It should be clear and focused, but not too narrow. For example, "I want to be known worldwide as a leader in digital media," or "I want to be known as a leader in understanding consumer behavior," or "I will be known as an innovator in Social Purpose." Keep it simple and so clear that if we ask you, you can tell us in a second. If it sounds lofty, that's ok. Start climbing the mountain.

#2 – How do I prefer to express myself? Make it easy on yourself. Pick one area and go for it. Don't overthink it. Start expressing yourself more.

#3 – What will I do to build momentum? If you want to write columns, it helps to write blog posts first. If you want to keynote, it helps to be on panels first. If you want to lead special events, it helps to author books first. Think of your work as practice that helps others discover your intelligence, so they can understand how to apply it in new ways.

#4 – Who can I partner with, either inside our network of firms or outside, to increase my brand relevance? Combine thoughts and have fun building new ideas with your friends. Think of ways to improve their positioning, not just yours.

#5 – When I talk with a client interested in thought leadership, what can I offer them next time we talk? Can you offer a column or ask to write a post together? Remember that most people in our positions rarely think beyond themselves. This creates a terrific opportunity for us.

Finally, think of where you want to make an impact. Here is the normal evolution of flow:

100% external – We do this to establish ourselves.

70% external/30% internal – Clients start to ask us to share our thoughts with their teams, run special innovation sessions, and do lunch 'n learns on key topics.

70% internal/30% external – Clients see a major advantage in talking with us privately with their teams, since they can hear new ideas sooner than their competitors. They gladly accept an opportunity to hear from us on key trends, new technology applications, and more.

The latter scenario leads to the newest opportunities. It just takes time to get there.

In summary, don't overthink thought leadership. Do think continually about how you can leverage what you know to open minds and open doors. Have confidence in yourself to figure out what's next a bit faster than your competitors. We're totally capable of doing so if we put our minds to it, literally.

And have fun!

CHAPTER 23

HOW TO EXPLORE NEW IDEAS

SEARCH MEDIA RELATIONS

"Not all those who wander are lost."

—J.R.R. Tolkien

It can feel like you're lost sometimes.

It's funny how certain topics just keep coming back to you. You know there is something there, so you start exploring what the opportunity might be.

Don't expect lots of support at this stage. You'll get some nods of interest, but few who join you. So, you continue to wander and explore.

To unlock your next ideas, look at current models and just assume we aren't hearing the whole story. For example, it always struck me that Google was so much more than a search engine. The question is what is it, and how does it apply to our clients?

Here is a sample of the thinking I put together while wandering like an Istari in *The Lord of the Rings*:

The Value of Google

Google is the most undervalued media platform in the world. We utilize Google to learn about a new product or service, conduct our own research, and often decide on our next steps for a topic of importance.

In our world of media, the 1:9:90 model has effectively demonstrated the importance of reaching the influencers (1 percent), the followers who often shape markets (9 percent), and the 90 percent of us who lurk and learn.

Traditionally, communications and marketing teams are excellent at identifying the 1 percent, who are prolific content creators, and we are "ok" at reaching the 9 percent of people who share content to inform their communities. Today, there is an unmet need related to how we reach the 90 percent of us who choose to learn by searching for information. It is worth noting that the 1 and 9 drive the narrative in the 90 percent, so this is a natural continuum of our workflow.

We view this unmet need as an opportunity to develop a new position centered on "search media relations."

Since search media relations is a new discipline in the world of communications and marketing, we have created this executive summary to explain the range of its importance.

DESCRIPTION (Six Key Areas)

How We Improve Campaigns – In our campaigns, we know who the influencers are, who to follow, and which media channels are most important. To improve, we can analyze what content, people, channels, and organizations appear for the top one hundred queries for our product, service, or company, and then create the equivalent of a Venn diagram to identify new actionable insights. For example, we will see that certain people are more influential than we first believed, or we can see which topics/content are being received when people search for the topic we care about.

The Supply Chain of Language – Keywords are the glue that enables a person searching via a query to find our story. Our goal is to continually identify the keywords that are driving the most search results for topics important to us and then ensure that all teams have these keywords. By including all teams that create websites, moderate social channels, create content, and advertise on the web, we are creating a "supply chain of language."

Reputational Strength or Fragility – We can determine the relative strength or fragility of our brand reputation in search results by conducting a series of simple analyses related to top queries for a product, service, or company (top one hundred queries), and then understanding the density of content for each query (number of results). If you have low results, it is easy for a new topic (pro or con) to enter the first screen. If we think of issues management, we now start to imagine how we can build strength for all areas where we may have vulnerabilities by proactively introducing positive content with the right keywords and methodically building a presence that is difficult to penetrate, whether it is a negative issue or a competitor. Overall, as the amount of content on any topic increases, the more difficult it is for new content to enter the first screen, which can build a protective digital barrier for our brands.

The Power of Q&As—We know humans think and act in finite terms. In studying their behavior worldwide for years, we realize that a community cannot think of more than two to four hundred questions about a topic important to us. Therefore, we want to proactively identify these questions, develop the best answers, and then share these Q&As digitally with appropriate links. Twitter is a great vehicle to do this since it caters to a Q&A format and has high impact on search results due to its open-source nature.

Competitor Review and Intelligence—We can routinely analyze our competitive set to understand where we have opportunities to reach their audience. We study where there are lower results and we can provide new content. If we remember that search often provides either a first impression or an important one in the sales process of a product or idea, it is important for us to find ways to move into the space of our competitors when people search for their keywords. Think long term and you can achieve the goal of penetrating the space of those you compete against.

Google is also a wealth of intelligence and can become a powerful listening platform. We can utilize analytic approaches, for example, to analyze the reputation of a brand or competitor over decades. We can go deep in understanding what matters in terms of content, influence, and channel at the zip code level. It is more a matter of the questions we want to answer than our capabilities if we choose to tap into the intelligence available from Google.

New Ways to Combine Intelligence—For example, why not combine the insights from a) Google, b) incoming sales questions, and c) call centers to determine another Venn diagram? If we know how people interact with us from all angles, we have the best perspective. We know customers will ask the same question in different ways in a 1:1 call versus asking a machine versus what they say when talking with a sales rep. Putting together this info leads to unique insights.

In this regard, we look at Google as the world's most trusted library with one catch. It indexes all content based on what is considered to be most relevant. So, it is the most trusted *and* relevant library.

KEY OUTCOMES

Here are a few examples of potential outcomes we can expect from a search media relations leader and an increased focus on this important area.

- **Right Narratives for Top Twenty Searches**—Think of this as a search media plan. We know what content and keywords we want to introduce into the market to impact the top searches important to us.
- **Improve Our Follower Strategy**—We identify new people and organizations that have influence via search. We add them to our follower list for our own social media channels.
- **Optimize Our Campaigns**—We identify people, media channels, topics, and organizations that we are either not reaching or not emphasizing in our existing outreach and update our approach based on what we see in key searches.
- **A New Way to Protect Our Reputation**—We identify where we have risk due to the fragility of our position, we keep track of where our competitors have similar issues, and we focus on building a presence that will act like a digital barrier when issues arise in the future. We also look at our corporate positions in important areas and determine how we can improve our search rank so that our strength of conviction matches our strength of position in search.

- **Use Right Language** – We check for which keywords are driving search results to understand the language important to our target audience, then check against our existing content. Something as simple as "car versus auto" makes a difference, as we know.
- **A Stronger SEO Strategy Makes SEM More Effective** – Marketers often joke that we use SEM to make up for poor SEO. Of course, if we are exceptionally strong in SEO, we are then able to use SEM surgically and focus more on specific areas of opportunity rather than making up for a poor SEO effort.
- **New Unmet Needs Are Discovered** – We can see trends earlier by watching how search queries shift in a category, which can impact the type of content and/or messaging we offer to the market.
- **Improves Owned Media** – A strong SEO presence always has content that links back to the appropriate page on our website, ensuring that our strength in SEO matches our strength in owned media.
- **Build Up the Long Tail** – We identify queries with important topics and lower results. They represent an opportunity for us to lead the first screen with our answers and narrative.
- **The Customer Journey** – By studying queries, we can estimate which phase of the marketing funnel our customers are in and how this shifts over time.
- **B2B Audience Expansion** – We identify key influencers and customers who are impacting our search results and reach out to them to participate in our earned and shared media. By doing so, we "borrow" their audience, who learns more about what we offer, impacting earned media, shared media, and organic search. This is a common tactic of select B2B companies.

What you see here are years of wondering and wandering in the fields of search. And there is a lot more ahead. This is just the beginning of that journey. The key is to document your path and continue to build on what you learn.

LEADERSHIP INSIGHT

Your Biggest Defeats Define Your Ability to Succeed

When I worked at Rhône-Poulenc Rorer (now Sanofi), our most important new drug was expected to be Taxotere, a new cancer drug at the time. The entire company was behind it, and we went to present to the US Food and Drug Administration's Oncologic Drugs Advisory Committee (ODAC) with high hopes, which were soon dashed as we were rejected.

We flew back to our headquarters in Collegeville, PA, and were immediately summoned to the boardroom with our chair and CEO. They asked what went wrong, did a quick diagnosis, and then pivoted the conversation to focus on what our next steps would be to gain approval. We walked out of the room feeling partly dejected and partly inspired and quickly realized that it was our job to define our future, period.

We regrouped, refiled, and soon enough, received a unanimous approval from ODAC. Taxotere went on to become one of the most important cancer drugs in history.

We could have given up and spent time lamenting. But we didn't. We became more determined.

That is what a successful attitude looks and feels like.

CHAPTER 24

THE BEST SALES ADVICE I EVER RECEIVED

"Starve your distractions, feed your focus."

—*anonymous*

I was asked to move from the headquarters of CIBA-GEIGY (now Novartis) in Summit, New Jersey, to become a sales representative at the age of twenty-seven. My only ask was for the company to give me the worst territory in the country, so I could see what impact I could make. It turned out to be Bradenton, Florida.

It was dead last and had been for years.

Eighteen months later, my territory was in the lead, and I was asked to go through district manager training, so I could oversee ten sales reps myself in the future. I was going to be taught how to manage colleagues who are all remote to ensure they were aligned with the goals of each brand and our company, so they could meet or exceed their sales goals.

I was all ears to understand what was most important to succeed in managing ten fairly independent, ambitious, and rather opinionated people—part of what makes a sales rep great at what they do.

It was here that I received the best sales advice in my career.

Here is the scenario:

You are managing ten sales representatives who each have their own territory and revenue goals, and their bonuses (and yours) are dependent on what you do individually and as a team. You sink or swim based on what you do in the field. No excuses. Numbers speak for themselves.

Of the ten, the makeup of the team looks like this.

- Two reps are absolute stars. Self-starters. Disciplined. Great results.
- Three reps are excellent. Dependable. Need guidance and they get there.
- Three reps are emerging. They won't surprise you either way. Might succeed, might not.
- Two reps are noisy. Complaining all the time. Everything is unfair to them. Very self-centered. They are pretty good at sales, but they are constantly harping on something.

Where do you spend your time?

The instinct of most leaders is to focus on the bottom. Spend most of your time with the two reps who are talented, but noisy, and spend the rest with the emerging reps, since maybe something will happen, and you want to make sure they make it. The top five reps receive far less attention or guidance because you believe they have their act together, and you don't have to worry about them.

Right answer? Nope. The exact wrong thing to do.

If you want to build the highest performing team, you do the opposite. You focus most of your time on the two superstars. Next, on the three excellent team members, and then on the emerging colleagues.

You spend the least amount of time on the noisy people. You remind yourself that every negative conversation is stealing time that could be spent on high performance leaders.

When you do this, your results improve and so does morale.

Why?

The two superstars have far more potential than you observe today. Your job is to unlock their potential. They could be future district managers or more. They can share marketplace learnings that help the entire team. You may be able to partner and open up new opportunities with customers. The list goes on.

Same for the next three team members. Focus here, and you will be surprised at what you can accomplish together.

The next three will keep improving as they watch closely what your top five do, particularly your top two. They mimic, learn from osmosis, and keep improving, so your time with the top team helps this next group.

The last two? They may get strong results, but they will still complain about headquarters, the latest sales aids, other people, vacation time, their bonus, how hard they work, and on and on. They will vent until the sun goes down and wake up ready to go again.

Your actions will make it clear that you have time for team members who are here to build the best team and be team players. You have close to zero time for those who work against those goals.

The results part is obvious. You will have stronger revenue results.

What is more subtle is how you lead. You lead by supporting those who choose to make a difference and desire to succeed. And those who create the noise realize it's time to mature professionally or move on. Or they can just find other people to complain to.

After getting that advice thirty-five years ago, it has been reinforced in every situation I have been involved in as a manager/leader.

And yet, it is human nature for leaders, particularly new ones, to worry about anyone who creates noise.

When this happens, remember the quote: "Starve your distractions, feed your focus."

If you do, you also unlock. If you don't, you'll be another mediocre manager.

CHAPTER 25

THE GROWTH OF A PRACTICE

THE EIGHT P'S DRIVING GROWTH

"Discipline is the bridge between goals and accomplishment."

—*Jim Rohn*

It is so easy as a leader to give out goals for the following year and then let your leaders know they need to meet those goals.

No real effort. Basic math. Pretty lazy.

It's one of the reasons why some firms don't grow as expected, or they grow in a direction they didn't expect.

Growth and discipline are cousins. And these cousins need a model that illustrates how to approach growth each year.

Think of your financial results as the "side effect" of the work you will do.

Experience has shown us that what works is a model we can all remember and measure against during the year. One example is our "8 P Model."

Here is a description to help illustrate the model. If you work in a service firm, this is created for you. If you work as a client, you can easily build a version that works inside a company. Not exact, but similar.

Our growth team plays an important role in how we shape our future via the growth of our portfolio of clients. We believe it is important to develop a plan and metrics that reflect on the importance of the eight P's of growth.

#1 – Pipeline – Our goal is to have a pipeline that is at least 50 percent of the value of our annual revenue on a discounted basis. Growth leaders will ensure that we are at 50 percent and are developing the next year's leads so that we can conduct the right outreach to build momentum in the current year and are setting up the next year concurrently. A two-year outlook.

#2 – Partners – We will win more often when we team up. We will gain more leads when we partner with experts outside of our network. Growth leaders are responsible for ensuring we have the right team at a pitch, so we maximize our chance to win. And great partners are always thinking about how they can identify the next opportunities together.

#3 – Product – We look at how to package our services to make them easier to sell. An "easy to sell" product has a) a clear name, b) a model that can be described in a paragraph or a slide, and c) an easy to share price or price range. You will also identify unmet needs, which can lead to the creation of new products.

#4 – Positioning – Thought leadership and related networking is done to either strengthen existing relationships and/or build new relationships. Growth leaders find ways to integrate current and future clients into our thought leadership activities (e.g., events, podcast, blog posts, etc.).

#5 – Pricing and Process – Clarity of pricing by product or service makes it easier to sell. Clarity of how we build an RFP or RFI response increases our chance to progress to the next level. The easier we make it to explain our pricing and develop budgets, the better. This is part financial and part process improvement.

#6 – Place – Our clients and talent drive where we have offices. If we are in the right places, it can increase our ability to take on new and sometimes larger assignments. What new offices will we start? How will geographic reach help us?

#7 – Portfolio – What do we want to build in three to five years? If a firm, what types of practices and clients do we want? If a practice, how many subsectors of this industry require unique expertise and teams? Who are the clients we want in each sector/subsector and why? This type of portfolio thinking can drive many of our decisions in P's 1-6.

#8 – Performance – What we do is qualitative and quantitative. It is easy to measure performance. Our winning percentage. The number of opportunities we must present. The value of our pipeline. Make the quantitative clear and then focus on the qualitative to get there.

When you are building your plan, ask what you are doing for each of the eight P's and ensure you have quantitative measures for each one. This will act as a strategic filter for you to build a successful growth strategy and achieve the results to back it up.

Then, throughout the year, check how you are doing. You will see where you are doing things well, which areas you tend to ignore, and where you need to do a better job.

Like any useful model, it is a temperature check on your efforts year round.

CHAPTER 26

THE SOFT SKILLS OF LEADERSHIP

"As we look ahead into the next century,
leaders will be those who empower others."
—*Bill Gates*

It is easy to get so focused on quantitative measures that we forget or more likely place less emphasis on the soft skills of leadership.

Think of it as being part of an orchestra. Every orchestra can have the same sheet music, but how they play together makes a world of difference. The soft skills of leadership involve our abilities to teach, unlock the capabilities of each individual and small team, and always have our eye on how we keep confidence high and our mindset focused.

The list of soft skills can be long and different depending on who is on your team, but here are five actions that are always important:

#1 – Osmosis – You stop and ask how your teammate is researching a topic, writing a post, or creating a spreadsheet, and you share one tip. You do this regularly, a tip at a time. It is one of the more powerful ways to share your knowledge. It is personal, shows you care, and truly helps.

#2 – Problem/Solution – When your team has a problem, you ask them to come to you with an articulation of the problem and a potential solution. Too often, teams are conditioned that it is ok to complain, so they do. No answers, just complaints. The best leaders don't accept this. They ask for a solution every time and will send you back to find one. This is a powerful mindset to have.

#3 – Questions – You know when to speak and share your insights and when to ask questions and listen. If you are always giving a sermon, you are creating way too much dependence on your "brilliance." Listen carefully and ask questions designed to open the minds of your team. And resist answering the question you just asked.

#4 – Sharing Credit – Assume anything good that happens occurs due to a team effort and be ready to accept failure on behalf of the team. That's right. Share credit but accept failure. As the leader, you are letting your team know you appreciate them and have their back.

#5 – Your Actions – How do you conduct a meeting? How do you handle a tough moment? How do you show respect for the delivery person? Every action you take as a leader sends a message about what you care about. All your inaction does the same.

I have found that if you are self-aware about what you are doing well and where you can improve, you will keep advancing in how you lead.

The mistake most leaders make is thinking, "Oh, I am already good at this." Just do yourself a favor, step back for a minute and remember that the best leaders on earth never say it. Only the insecure or clueless leaders say it.

You can make such a big difference in people's lives by doing this well. Give it your best effort.

CHAPTER 27

THE PSYCHOLOGY OF FORECASTING

"Don't wait for inspiration. It comes while one is working."
—Henri Matisse

A quote from an artist is perfect for a chapter that involves how we look at our blank canvas each year that we refer to as our forecast.

How you look forward is a direct reflection of how you operate in the world every day. It's more of a mirror into your business soul than you might think.

A forecast can be for your firm or practice or a single client. The same dynamics occur.

Some of us prefer not to think too much about a forecast. What we have now is just fine. We are in control of our efforts, and that works for us. When asked, we give vague answers about next year's growth. We hedge and avoid these questions.

Some of us are willing to sign up for the basic goal. We are not sure how we will achieve the growth ahead, but we are team players. The forecast was largely given to us, since we didn't want to go out on a limb and be bold in our prediction, but we accept what was given and will probably hit our goal.

Some of us imagine a goal that gets many leaders uncomfortable in its boldness. It's imagining a growth scenario we may have never achieved before. You can tell when new ideas are viewed as important, often by how other leaders try to throw cold water on the concept. Many of us resist change more than we realize.

We can think of more, but these are the most common buckets we often fit in. It is worth noting that we evolve over the years based on our experience, so there is no "right place" to be today.

Knowing all of this, let's assume you are a leader who wants to grow the firm more than it has in its history and you are spending way too much time convincing the first two groups to think bigger. What can you do?

Well, if you are leading the firm or practice, you build what I call a "shadow forecast." You build one forecast that represents the achievable goals for the firm and a shadow forecast. For example, an achievable forecast of 10 percent growth in fee income and ebit (earnings before income and tax) and a shadow forecast that will achieve 20 percent growth. You then budget and plan against the 10 percent plan, but you identify the moves you need to make to reach 20 percent and make them throughout the year if the budget allows.

If you are a skeptic, you may ask why this simple process works.

It works because most of us don't believe a firm can grow until they see it actually happen. Once they do, their skepticism decreases until the new growth rate becomes the norm. They often become future champions of this new norm, in fact.

The leader of the firm must be the artist in the room who sees the whole canvas today. They can imagine what it will look like when complete and then act accordingly.

This is why Henri Matisse's quote is so accurate to forecasting. Your inspiration and confidence in your firm's growth will come while working.

Do your best to imagine your canvas and then start painting. Today.

LEADERSHIP INSIGHT

What Would Barry Do?

When I was on the Huntington's Disease Society of America Board along with Michael Roth, we would raise money and make decisions on where to spend money to advance research and support patients and caregivers.

At that time, a board member named Barry was with us. Barry had active HD, which is a disease that can cause a person to lose control of their limbs and result in sudden jerking motions, among other conditions.

Every time we made a decision, we felt Barry's presence in the boardroom and knew it better be the best decision to support Barry and everyone else in the community.

When you are deciding on behalf of others, imagine they are in the room with you. Every time.

CHAPTER 28

THE SIGNALS CLIENTS GIVE US

"I can't get no satisfaction, I can't get no satisfaction.
'Cause I try, and I try, and I try, and I try.
I can't get no, I can't get no."
— *The Rolling Stones*

As the story goes, Mick Jagger woke up one morning in 1965, saw a cassette tape, and played it. It was Keith Richards saying, "I can't get no satisfaction," followed by forty minutes of snoring. Today, that song is the third most popular song on Spotify for the Stones.

Those of us who are considered great at client service live by this phrase. It doesn't mean we are unhappy, but we are perpetually on the lookout for our clients' signals. Yes, we ensure our work is excellent and stay in touch with the client, but we keep hearing someone somewhere saying, "I can't get no satisfaction."

It's similar to being an athlete. You are taught at an early age that even though you are playing well, there is another kid in the next town who practices more and is going to beat you the next time you play.

You live with this awareness that an issue may be occurring that you don't know about. A competitor may be making a play for your business, and you are unaware. A client team may be about to be disbanded and impact you. There are many ways "satisfaction" can be impacted.

So, what do the best client service leaders do with all these unknowns?

Well, they don't fall asleep like Keith Richards. Instead, they listen for unsaid cues.

There are many, but the five below illustrate the point.

THE AGENCY PERSPECTIVE

Silence beyond the work – You are doing the work; everything is working. But you are not engaging with any real intensity with your client. It's not truly silent, but there is nothing extra going on. It is a sign, perhaps, of a relationship that is going fine, but could get stale.

Incoming questions – How often is your client team calling you with questions? How often do they call to talk about issues that do not directly relate to your exact workflow?

Regularity of meetings – How often do you meet in person? Are you going to the client? Are they coming to visit you?

New team members – How are your new team members gelling with the client team? How are new members in the client team impacting how you work, and are you building strong relationships?

Extracurricular activities – What do you do outside of work together? Think about the last year and the current year. Are you providing value beyond the normal relationship?

Every one of these areas contains a lot of subtlety. If you ask your team, they will tell you all is great, and everyone loves each other. But it is your job as a leader to read between the lines and wonder.

Below are five responses, in return, that I thought of when I was a client.

THE CLIENT PERSPECTIVE

Silence – Sometimes it means we trust the firm we have hired. Other times, it means we see them as productive workers, but not much more. Determining which you are is important.

Incoming questions – I always asked the people I trusted for advice. I did not call most agency leaders, because if I did, they would try to upsell me, direct me to another expert, or do something that was a waste of time. I called the people who could brainstorm with me.

Regularity of meetings – It is always better to meet in person. Too many agencies didn't ask. The ones that did visit often received extra time. We had different conversations, and they walked out with new assignments or a new idea for the future. Trust is built in person.

New team members – When a new team member joins, get to know them. Make time to learn their approach and ideas and understand their career path. Never ignore them and treat them differently based on rank or positioning in a meeting, as that can start to unravel a relationship. Some agencies always find ways to embrace the newcomers and build stronger relationships. Embrace every new team member, and you will be in good shape.

Extracurricular activities – Business friends look out for each other. They talk us up for board positions or recommend us as keynotes for a conference and much more. I would say most of the "best stuff" I have done is due to a friend in the industry who looked out for me. I do the same in return. That builds special relationships.

CHAPTER 29

THE TOP TEN WAYS TO BUILD A GREAT CLIENT RELATIONSHIP

"Successful people are always looking for opportunities to help others. Unsuccessful people are always asking, 'What's in it for me?'"

—*Brian Tracy*

I remember my first days as a new pharmaceutical sales representative for CIBA-GEIGY. I am not sure any of my customers were aware I existed or cared if I visited them. My first interactions with clients as an assistant account executive for Carl Byoir & Associates were similar.

In both situations, what I realized was that my job is to find ways to be of value to my customers and clients. Every interaction.

Not a single customer or client was wondering if I would be successful. They were all, rightfully, wondering how they could provide more value to their constituents, as it should be.

In our world, the best relationships are tied directly to clients viewing us as providing the most value every day. We are dependable. Whenever we put ourselves before their needs, that's when trouble starts.

Here is what I have learned from working with some of the most talented people in our industry. A special top ten on how to build a productive and valuable relationship.

#1 – Do exactly what you said you would do. If you commit to an outcome, you make it happen. The only reason it may not happen is if there are variables completely outside of your control. But still, you are the one who is knocking down the wall to still try to get it done.

FIRM GROWTH

#2 – Learn and think like your client. Learn what they read and do the same. Read the investor relations decks and think like an investor. Read about their competitors. Understand products and services completely. It's what your client is doing to keep up in their own environment. Keep up and be an intellectual partner, not just a doer of activities.

#3 – Identify and solve future problems or create new opportunities. If you know a client's business inside and out, you really aren't "selling" when you offer new ideas. You're anticipating their needs and offering solutions that your client appreciates. This is when organic growth becomes powerful.

#4 – Build a great team with similar acumen. We all know the weakest link can define us. Ask your team to join you on the journey to be the best partner. Don't allow for anyone to be "partly" on board. Like a brand's reputation, it can be lost quickly if the wrong actions are taken. Same for teams.

#5 – No surprises. Who likes a surprise? The answer is not too many people. Clients never want to be surprised by any aspect of our relationship with them. Even if it is positive. Great partners share information in a fluid manner.

#6 – Succession plan for your team. Will you stay on this account for the remainder of your life? Not likely since you may be promoted or just need a break. Who is your next in line, and are you doing all you can to position this person with your client? It is a tremendous compliment to a senior leader when a client feels comfortable with your #2, and you are not needed as much. This allows both of you to grow.

#7 – Be available 24/7/365. Most clients don't call us in the evenings or on weekends, since they also like to have a life outside of work, but if they need us, they need us. Always be available by phone. Never put on an "out of office" message. If you really are indisposed, ensure your client knows who to call in a pinch.

#8 – Assume your work will get stale and refresh. When we work multiple years with the same client, it is important to routinely challenge ourselves internally to ensure our work is fresh and we aren't providing the same counsel and ideas as last time, since it is easier to continue than evolve.

#9 – Every touchpoint matters. How will your client be received when they visit your office? How does the invoice arrive to their company? How do you share new ideas? How do you communicate staff updates? Every time you have a potential touchpoint, ask if you are doing it in a way that you would be pleased if you were the client.

#10 – Be aware, but not part of client politics. Every organization with more than one human can say they have their moments. Larger organizations always have some level of what we call "politics." It is good to be aware of reality, but it is bad to spend your time joining in and gossiping, lamenting, and talking yourself into a state. Be the breath of fresh air and the team they can count on any and every time.

You will note that all ten points are relationship oriented. When I was a client myself, I assumed the best of my agency teams until proven otherwise. Often, you could not directly tell if an agency was veering off course, but you could see signs—a lack of new ideas, high team turnover (and a lack of communications about it), too much time to return calls and emails, and other actions that seem mundane but add up.

The best teams keep up with your business, and you feel like they are an extension of your own inside team. This is the ultimate place to be.

Great teams and relationships take work, which is why we spend so much time on how to build client excellence.

I will end with a simple personal checkpoint.

If you wake up every morning and think of how you will add value to your client(s) today, then you are highly likely to have a distinguished career in consulting. If you wake up and just think about your workflow and your day, well, you may do ok, but you aren't likely to lead the way in the future.

This is an area where anyone with the right attitude can become great at building relationships. It's all up to you.

CHAPTER 30

WHY RANKINGS AND AWARDS MATTER

"Winning doesn't always mean being first. Winning means you're doing better than you've ever done before."

—*Bonnie Blair*

Spoken like a winner of five Olympic gold and one bronze medals. Speed skater Bonnie Blair knew that improving is what counts. If you keep improving, you have the chance to win the gold.

Clients want to work with firms that are continually improving themselves, and individuals like to join firms that are intent on winning.

Rankings are a way to show our progress, often via financial results and sometimes by peer reviews.

Awards illustrate the power of our work.

If you choose not to participate, you are either accepting the status quo or maybe you won't like the results you may see.

Think of rankings and awards as a mirror on your progress. The world doesn't stop spinning if you win or lose. But it does show if you are making progress.

Be ok with embracing how your industry views you. And have fun sharing your firm's success.

By the way, don't forget to share the credit with your clients. You couldn't do any of this without them.

CHAPTER 31

TREES OF GROWTH

"The aim of marketing is to know and understand the customer so well the product or service fits him and sells itself."

—*Peter Drucker*

Every business talks about organic growth. How will our current business grow to keep up with our rising costs and drive our business forward?

I have always looked at organic growth as the ultimate vote of confidence in a supporting firm. After all, clients are only going to give more work to those firms they trust and expect to create excellent outcomes.

So we all agree organic growth is good, but then it becomes a noisy discussion.

The lack of discpline in organic growth plans is astonishing, which is why we use what we call the Trees of Growth.

A tree takes time to grow. It has many branches. It's not easy to climb. It's a great metaphor.

The Trees of Growth model is logical and just requires the usual dash of discipline, patience, a great track record with the client, and ideas to match.

Here's our approach:

> First, always ensure you are absolutely nailing your client assignment. Every day, week, month, year. Without that, this whole discussion is mute, so you could say that great organic growth really starts with an awesome team doing the day-to-day work. Thank you!

Now, thinking as the clients we once were, we were always wondering if our best partners had more answers in the following areas:

New Services – What can you do beyond communications? How about marketing, for example?

New Geographies – You are great in the US. What about the UK?

New Functions – The communications function loves the team. What can you do for our events team or our sales team?

Next up are clients themselves. Our relationships with our best clients should really become lifelong "Biz-Friendships." Here is where you can also differentiate yourself via:

New Relationships – Can we help you join a board in an area you are passionate about? Can we team up on a special committee in an organization we both belong to?

Special Education – If our firm is expected to understand the future of technology, for example, why don't we come in and offer a "top ten trends that will impact your team" type of lunch 'n learn? How we decide to share our expertise in new ways matters to our client.

Thought Leadership – Can we write a column together? Include them in a book we are writing? Invite them to a webinar or do a podcast together?

Clients also give us a gift we seldom think about.

We are becoming experts in their marketplace. Where else could we apply this knowledge? We may be able to build a roster of clients in a certain space, e.g., insurance or digital health, and start a small practice.

Finally, we have the ultimate compliment. Our client is promoted to their next job and decides to take us with them.

How well do we keep in touch with our "client alumni," and what do we do to make that real?

It all sounds easy, so I ask that you hold a meeting and ask your team to answer these questions for your top clients. If they can answer with clarity, specificity, and a great track record for each area, then you have a phenomenal and rare team. More likely you'll hear lots of discussion and realize it is less fact-laden than you wish.

Easy enough to improve. Just takes discipline, patience, a great track record, and ideas to match.

LEADERSHIP INSIGHT

What Do You Do When Someone Says You Can't Do Something?

I was told I could not be hired by my first firm, since they didn't hire out of college.

I was told I should not go into pharma, since I didn't know science.

I was told if I went into sales, I could fail and be fired and forgotten about.

I was told I was not good enough to be director of product communications and would fail.

I was told I didn't know consulting and would not make the transition from corporate to agency.

I was told I shouldn't go to a small firm to help them build, since there were much better opportunities for me.

What happened?

Carl Byoir & Associates hired me out of school. I flourished at CIBA-GEIGY and learned product communications. I turned the worst territory into the #1 territory in sales. I was promoted from director to global VP at Rhône-Poulenc Rorer. We created GCI Health in my first agency gig, which is now in the top thirty worldwide. I helped Real Chemistry start its launch phase of growth for a firm that is now nearly $600MM in revenue.

In each case, I heard these naysayers and decided to ignore them. I listened to the leaders, friends, and family who believed in me and moved full speed ahead.

There will always be people who tell you that you aren't good enough. It's your choice to listen or ignore them. Obviously, I recommend the latter.

CHAPTER 32

WHAT DOES INTEGRATION REALLY MEAN?

"If you want to lift yourself up, lift up someone else."
—*Booker T. Washington*

When I was a kid, I would occasionally walk into the family room and ask my parents, "What should we do?" like they would somehow know what a ten-year-old boy wanted to do. They would look at me and say, "Why don't you go out and play with the other kids? You'll figure it out."

Sure enough, we would gather the other kids in the neighborhood, and we would decide on what game we would play together. It could be hide-and-seek or soccer or something created on the spot.

A solution had been found by reaching out to friends and talking through what we could do together.

Hours later, we heard our parents shouting in the distance for us to come home for dinner. The time had flown by. We were having a great time, but we reluctantly finished up and walked home or ran, depending on who our parents were.

None of us realized what we were doing, but in reality, we were figuring out how to listen to each other and develop a solution we could all benefit from. We just didn't think of it in those terms. And if some consultant had magically popped in and said this is what was happening, we would have said, "Who are you? You're weird," and gone right back to our game.

Fast forward to the business world. Isn't that what integration really is?

A figure above us doesn't tell us what to do. Rather, we get together with our friends, who may have different skills, be in different firms, or work with different clients, and we think about what we can do that will be worthwhile.

Then the magic happens.

By listening to each other and staying focused on what our clients need, we develop a new product, service, or model that is so useful that our clients appreciate our work, we love applying our new knowledge, and the time just flies by. That is, until we hear a call in the distance to "come home," only this time it may be to solve another problem or create a new opportunity. We will always be asked to "come home" and figure things out all over again. C'est la vie.

Remember our childhood when we integrate. Be open minded. Listen to our friends. Figure out solutions that can work in practice. Have fun. Keep it simple.

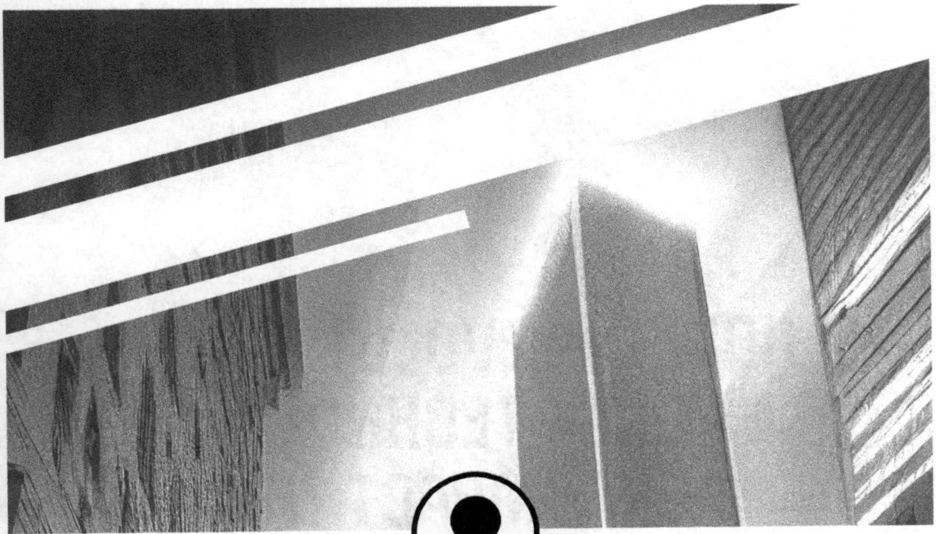

INNOVATION

CHAPTER 33

HOW THE EVOLUTION OF MEDIA & TECHNOLOGY WILL IMPACT THE CURRENT AND FUTURE ROLE OF THE CCO

"Leadership is an ever-evolving position."

—*Mike Krzyewski*

In chapter 11, we talk about how to visualize the future of a position and its day-to-day issues to better relate to how we can provide value.

Every now and then, we are asked, as leaders, to envision the future. For example, we may be asked, "What will the future role of your position as chief communications officer be, and what trends are important to know?"

It's a big question. Often a bit intimidating. The way I approach these questions is to think about the world we work in and flush out the trends that truly matter.

In the summary below, I envision how the media world is evolving, how technology is impacting this change, and what it means to a CCO.

EXECUTIVE SUMMARY

In this executive summary, we explore three key areas important to the career development of current and future chief communication officers. In each area, we provide examples to show the extent of change, knowing there is a longer list ahead of us.

Most Important Global Media Trends

Technology innovation creates new opportunities for the world to consume, interact with, and benefit from content. Here are examples where we can take our understanding of change and turn it into opportunities for CCOs:

Attention spans – We know via billions of data points that we make decisions on content in one to two seconds. Consumers worldwide are pouring through social media, music choices, gaming decisions, and other actions that deeply reinforce short attention spans. We also know that if we gain one's attention, they will spend time learning more.

Action: *How we create content needs to be re-evaluated, so we reach our audience. How do we apply the journalist pyramid, as it relates to text, images, headlines, and other ways to gain attention? What are the most common errors we make when we misjudge how the subconscious mind of the consumer works?*

Audience architecture – Via analytics, we can see exactly how our audience interacts online, who they respect, what content they prefer, which words trigger behavior, and much more. It is important that we understand our audience before we create campaigns, so we can align our narrative with their needs.

Action: *Understanding how to effectively build profiles, utilize custom algorithms, and identify how an audience shapes a market will be a key skill of the communications team. We want to know the 1 percent who create content, the 9 percent who share content, and the 90 percent who lurk and learn from the 1 and 9.*

Search media relations—The most undervalued media platform on earth is search engines. Google commands one-third of digital ad revenue worldwide and is the second most visited platform in the world. Via analytics, we can see which people, organizations, and topics show up for key search queries, which shows us how our audience will discover our story.

Action: *Expand how we prepare for a narrative/campaign, so we know who we want to reach to report on our story, who will share our story, and who is important via search queries that we may not be working with today.*

How we learn from social media—TikTok is an excellent example, since it is now the #1 most visited platform in the world. TikTok illustrates how new applications of software make it easy to create content. For example, a TikTok video teaches us how to communicate in fifteen to sixty seconds. You can add augmented reality effects, create a video from multiple photos using premade templates, select audio to add to the video, record at different speeds, soften lines and smooth out facial complexion, change lighting and color, and share it all live.

Action: *We need to ensure that our teams are as fluent in creating content on any social media channel as our audience. If we are not aligned, we will continue to create content that looks like a company or brand trying way too hard.*

Software Solutions Are Finally Ready to Improve the Efficiency of Communications

We are all tired of hearing from the nearly ten thousand MarTech solutions that often border more on the side of hype than hope. However, we are now witnessing a relative maturity of software solutions that are leading to new applications for communicators. Here are a few examples:

From town hall to global community—We can now build private mobile apps that allow us to share audio, video, text, and white papers in specific channels, e.g., "Town Hall" or "Product Launch ABC." We can encourage our employees to share their own content and converse within the channel. We can provide surveys or simple questions to learn more. Imagine a CEO's Town Hall being the spark that leads to learning worldwide on the important topics of the quarter and year.

One person can have the impact of thirty—Imagine shooting three to four hours of video on a key topic, turning the video into hundreds of blocks (one to three sentences each) and then being able to create thousands of personalized videos from this one session. Imagine writing text that can be translated into 350+ languages and shared worldwide. One person in your department could become the global communicator at a level that would have normally required agencies worldwide and/or a team of thirty.

Content creation is rapidly changing—Generative AI is making it possible to improve how we create content. Understanding how technology can accelerate and improve our content creation will change how we utilize our teams and their supportive firms.

Overall action—It is important for CCOs to routinely review which technological applications can advance their agenda. This requires a formal approach on how to assess, understand, and experiment with new solutions.

Bad Actors Are Advancing Faster than the Fortune 1000 (thus far)

Bad actors are not worried about rules, regulations, or social norms, so their ability to innovate will always occur at a rapid pace. The big change is that the digital world is making it easier than ever for bad actors to impact our organizations, communities, and citizens in seven important ways: ransomware, illicit drug flow, counterfeit products and services, disinformation to throw us off balance, extremist behavior to recruit vulnerable people, censorship, and interfering with elections. These actions are directed at us from groups that range from organized crime groups to adversarial countries to individual extremists.

The best way to protect the reputation of our organization and the communities we serve is to understand how bad actors work. For example, what does the supply chain of a ransomware attack look like from St. Petersburg, Russia, to your IT system? Or how does illegal fentanyl move with ease into the US via use of social media, forums, and the dark web?

We also need to shift from platforms that listen to platforms that provide us with intelligence that we can act on to understand our vulnerabilities.

Overall, when we look at the actions of bad actors, they can impact companies, communities, citizens, and countries—the four C's.

Action: It is important for us to understand exactly how bad actors work. Then, we can develop the best readiness plans, engage in the most effective training, and identify the right intelligence platforms to keep as ahead as one can be in our world.

You get the point. When you take the time to think through how a function or the world around it is evolving, it helps us understand how to best align in the future.

Take the time to think aloud, write it down, and imagine what you will do differently as a result.

CHAPTER 34

SOFTWARE ALLOWS US TO DREAM OF A NEW FUTURE

"Sometimes I believe in as many as six impossible things before breakfast."
—*Alice, from* Alice in Wonderland

Think of software as a rebel. A way to unlock innovative ideas. A way to make our crazy ideas real.

If you do, you will be surprised at how you can innovate by partnering with the best software developers and their creations.

The hard part is imagining what is possible.

The way I approach innovation with software is to think like Alice and imagine crazy things, some of which come true.

Here are a few examples from software companies I am familiar with:

Imagine one person doing the work of thirty—Iternal Technologies has built a software platform that can organize video, for example, into "blocks," so that you can hold a one-hour video session and then create dozens or hundreds of personalized videos. You can do the same for text, slides, and reports.

Imagine having your entire intranet in your pocket—Aimcast has created a platform that enables us to build channels for the CEO, brand launch, or division, where we can share our views, listen to leaders, and receive new content, all in a private mobile app.

Imagine getting 10x the views of your stories—Shorthand has provided a new way to build highly engaging stories that can lead to, in some cases, 10x higher views than stories written in a traditional format.

Imagine helping to reach new communities via new media models—Ideas Beyond Borders is literally translating the world's information into Arabic to reach twenty-two countries in the Middle East and the Arabic-speaking population worldwide. What started as a translation exercise has turned into a new style of media platform.

Imagine protecting those who are oppressed with new tools to circumvent censorship—Psiphon is one of those tools developed by the University of Toronto to improve one's safety when receiving content in places where oppression exists and censorship is expected.

And the list goes on.

Our job is to think of the big idea. What do our clients and our world need?

If we know the unmet needs of our world, software can help us find solutions that scale.

We need each other. The best software engineer is only as good as the problem they will solve and the team that will help them share their creation.

LEADERSHIP INSIGHT

Innovation Is Lonely

We were working night and day to launch a new idea community for Dell called IdeaStorm. It represented a new way to gain insights from our customers and employees, so our designers and developers could assess those ideas and help us align more closely with our audience.

The day before we launched, an executive came into my double-wide cube and said that this was a bad idea, it should be killed, and I was jeopardizing the company. My team asked what was happening, and I said, "Oh, nothing, just received some helpful feedback," and we continued on.

IdeaStorm was a success because it helped our teams apply learnings from our audience. Later, Starbucks asked if they could replicate our platform for My Starbucks Idea, so we agreed to transfer our knowledge. The original idea, by the way, was one we had borrowed from Salesforce.com. We were just paying it forward.

This is one of many examples I have where we are at the forefront of innovation and receive feedback that is, let's say, not so helpful. But you persevere because we know innovation is lonely.

Success, on the other hand, is a big room with lots of participants.

Power on.

CHAPTER 35

THE ART OF BEING SIMPLE

"Simple can be harder than complex; you have to work hard to get your thinking clean to make it simple. But it's worth it in the end because once you get there, you can move mountains."

—*Steve Jobs*

I learned a trick working for CEOs like Dan Vasella (Novartis), Michael Dell, and Rob Cawthorn (Rhône-Poulenc Rorer). I wrote down the topics I needed answers for on a three-by-five card and stuck it in my back pocket. Whenever I had a few extra minutes with a CEO, I could get right to the point and get answers that might otherwise take weeks to get.

I also realized that I ain't busy. They ARE busy! And this has led to a lifetime of learning to understand how to make things simple. Here are seven key learnings I have adopted over the years, with the caveat that all these ideas are ones I learned from my peers, so thank you.

The Index Card—If you write down the key topics you want to discuss with your leader, you will be ready to run down that list without ever looking at it. Leaders always have time for people who help them make quick and efficient decisions.

The Answer First Slide—Bain Consulting created this approach, which starts with giving the answer first! The slide outlines the answer, which serves as the foundation for your solution and what is involved in achieving your goal. What I have found is that if you can't outline your approach in one slide, you need to spend more time fine tuning your answer. At Dell, if you didn't do this, you didn't get to pass go.

The Five W's—Turns out the five W's (who, what, when, where, why) are the best questions to ask when evaluating a problem or an opportunity. If you take time to do this, you quickly see what is missing and/or know how to best articulate the next steps.

The Strategic Filter—For recurring activities, take the time to build out the three to five questions you need to answer before you get started. For example, if you are asked to launch a new product, go through your list upfront.

The One Slide Model—When creating a media model, such as how a market is shaped, if you can show how it works in one slide (e.g., the 1:9:90 media model), it can then scale in an organization, which means any team member anywhere in the world can easily understand the model. If you can understand, repeat, and share a model anywhere in the world, it is real. If you can't, you have work to do.

The One Pager—The advertising brief doesn't work well in my view. However, if you spend the time to write a one-pager articulating the vision for a new assignment, it clarifies for everyone what you hope to achieve, and it can be challenged. You can't challenge an ad brief, since it is often hard to figure out what we really think.

The Three-to-Five-Page Narrative—When you are building a new company, practice, or offering of substance, take the time to do what Amazon.com has done for years. Write a three-to-five-page narrative articulating why this should happen and share it with your fellow decision-makers for discussion. We too often rely on a slide deck or the goodwill of colleagues rather than writing it all down and seeing if it hangs together. If it does, great. If it doesn't, well, you saved time.

The key across the board is that simplicity is created when preparation is focused and strategic.

People who respect our time and improve decision-making are always welcome.

CHAPTER 36

WHEN DOES A MODEL BECOME REAL?

"Fact is, inventing an innovative business model is often mostly a matter of serendipity."

—Gary Hamel

The US government asked Kip Knight, Ed Tazzia, and a host of other smart people to envision a curriculum that would teach US government leaders how to tell powerful stories, combat disinformation, and more.

The team, which I am part of, kept evolving how it shared insights and developed a model of storytelling called the ABCDE Model.

It took off and is now a standard of how to discipline yourself to build powerful narratives.

The ingredients were all common knowledge. The model is simple. And yet it resonates.

Part of our master plan? Hardly. More like serendipity as Gary Hamel said.

What I would add to Gary's quote is that leaders must be smart enough to know when a model has potential and, quite frankly, when it doesn't. It is from here that we can turn a model into a platform.

We have seen this with the 1:9:90 media model. We have seen it with Audience Architecture. We have seen it with the ABCDE Model.

All simple models that require discipline to do well. All serve as strategic filters to keep at your side in the years ahead. And none of them require a PhD to explain.

We are all capable of building models that can make a difference. But if we are honest, we don't know yet which one is next.

THE ABCDE MODEL

The ABCDE Communication Model Grid *(with definitions)*	
Audience	Who you are trying to persuade (defined by demographics, behavior, attitudes, psychographics, etc.)?
• Audience Insight	Based on consumer research and analysis, what do you already know about your target audience that will be helpful in creating a persuasive communication campaign?
Behavioral Objectives	What exactly do you want your target audience to do based on this communication campaign?
Content	
• Benefit	What are you promising your target audience will get in return for the behavior you are advocating? Bottom line, what's in it for them (especially from an emotional POV)?
• Reason to Believe	Why should the target audience believe you can deliver the benefit you have promised them (i.e. endorsement, mechanism of action, ingredients, product/service attributes, etc.)?
• Tone/Character	What is the personality, attitude, and look/feel of your message (expressed in three words or less)?
Delivery—Media	Which online and offline media channels are you going to use to get your message out (e.g., Facebook ads, YouTube videos, print ads, PR campaign, TV commercials, etc.)?

(continues on the next page)

THE ABCDE MODEL *(continued from the previous page)*

Delivery—Message	What's the overall message you are going to be delivering to your target audience?
• On Brand	How does this communication campaign tie into and leverage your overall brand image?
• Recognizable	What is in this campaign that will make it easy for your target audience to quickly identify it with your brand?
• Simple	Is your overall message clear and simple enough that the target audience will be able to understand it quickly and easily?
• Attention Grabbing	What will be included in your communication campaign that will get the attention of your target audience?
Evaluation	What metrics are you going to use to evaluate the overall success of this communication campaign? Over what time period?

CHAPTER 37

LEARNING WORLDWIDE TO APPLY LOCALLY

THE FUTURE OF INFLUENCERS— A CONVERSATION WITH UKRAINIAN LEADERS

"Think globally, act locally."

—*said all of us*

Finding opportunities to speak outside your comfort zone can reinforce what is important and push you towards new ideas.

One of the more interesting ways to do this is to take global learnings and then apply them to an important local situation. If the ideas are useful, you can go from global to local. However, if the ideas are too far up in the clouds, you can't figure out the pragmatic responses.

It's a great exercise.

Below is an example of how I applied this thinking to a discussion with peers in Eurasia prewar.

MY SUMMARY

I had an opportunity to keynote at the Influencers Hub Ukraine Conference on "The Future of Influencers" to address leaders within the second-largest country by size and eighth largest in population in Europe (41.5 million people).

What a timely topic! How we build influence is critical to how we shape public opinion, instill the values important to the country, and counter disinformation.

The future of influence is being shaped by the tectonic shifts occurring in our habits as consumers of media. Here are two examples:

Our attention spans are one to three seconds. We decide whether we like new content so quickly, often on our phone, that how we create and present content makes the difference.

People we respect are replacing "authority figures" as trustworthy We tend to trust the people who are consistently informing us every day. This means that influencers in social media can build more trust and relevance in our lives than ever before. This can be good and bad, of course, depending on who it is.

After sharing a few global media models, I discussed five new ways for influencers to build relevance and reach. The leaders of media will likely embrace most of these models soon.

#1 – When we personalize content, we connect with our audience. When you study the top YouTube stars worldwide, for example, they are all excellent at "narrating life." They share their thoughts in a personal manner, which builds trust through their authenticity. They don't expect you to sit still and watch a video.

#2 – The next great news anchor will be in social media. As TV wanes worldwide, we realize most people get their news via social media, e.g., Facebook. What if a news reporter took the time to give a personal 60–120 second update every day for their Facebook channel with a link to a summary of the news? That could work. Hoping people will watch more news on TV won't work.

#3 – The next CNN will be within message platforms. Imagine setting up news groups in a thousand plus places within a single message platform to reach citizens in a given language, region, or worldwide. Crazy? Just as crazy as CNN thinking an Atlanta-based cable TV station would one day be in hotel rooms and airports worldwide. In fact, this is already happening in Telegram, for example.

#4 – The most important media platform on earth is gaming. The question is how do we become relevant within a game or a gaming platform/ecosystem versus simply advertising to it? This can include game mods, where we take an existing game, keep the mechanics the same, and change the narrative to join the journey to counter disinformation or change the climate. It is important for companies and brands to learn how to build relevance within the gaming community.

#5 – Imagine if one influencer could do the work of thirty worldwide. This is where software and media come together to create breakthroughs. It is quietly happening now. One influencer could, for example, spend one day creating video segments on a topic, let software organize and tag it, and then be able to create hundreds or even thousands of videos, in multiple languages, via one day of work.

The real headline is that how we define influence is evolving. It is important we keep up with how our media consumption habits are changing and how technology is creating new ways to communicate. We need to combine those with the ability to think outside the box.

As we like to say, the great ideas already exist. We just need to connect the dots and make them happen.

CHAPTER 38

WHAT MATTERS TO BE IN THE 1 PERCENT?

"The key to leadership today is influence, not authority."

—*Ken Blanchard*

We openly wonder how certain people gain so much influence in our digital world.

We call them the 1 percent since they are prolific content creators or contributors. They are part of the 1:9:90 model of media (9 percent share, 90 percent of us lurk and learn).

It is actually not a mystery why they have influence, since we also build algorithms that tell us exactly how they shape markets and who trusts them. From here, it becomes straightforward.

It is consistency, trust, and relevance. Let's break down all three with examples.

Consistency—We know from thousands of analyses that celebrities are almost never in the top fifty influencers for a major brand or company. This is due to a lack of consistency (and perhaps the other two attributes), so they may get attention for a moment, but it doesn't last. Contrast that with the person who creates content in a consistent manner on which you can depend. Consistency forms habits, and habits lead us to favor certain people.

It is worth noting that celebrities may have large audiences, but ask yourself how much real crossover there is between your core audience and theirs? If it's there, fair enough, but this is often not the case.

Trust – We tend to trust those who are in front of us with information we care about more often. This is why an Instagram or YouTube influencer often has far higher reach and relevance than our favorite news anchor. In fact, it's often not even close. The top influencer on TikTok has an audience that is 100x the size of CNN Prime Time. A pretty big difference that we consistently see. Why? Part of it is availability bias. When we see someone continually and like what they say, we trust them more. This is great if you are a social media influencer. It's bad if people are being misinformed or disinformed. Understanding the psychological models involved helps us see what is happening.

Relevance – Many years ago, we realized that a news outlet is just a news outlet. It is the reporters inside it that matter, and they all have different views, audience reach, and impact in the marketplace. So, for example, we can analyze all the reporters for a key outlet who might cover our company and then rank which ones have the most influence and why. Then, we look at who we were getting stories with and why that may be happening. We may not be reaching out to the right journalists. Same for other outlets. Fast forward to today, and journalists who lead know their digital presence must be strong or they are writing into the wind.

Another area worth thinking about is how people go from being interesting to being in the 1 percent.

One way is to understand the trends that matter to the audience you are targeting and ensure you write/talk on these topics.

A second way is to understand who your 9 percent are or could be and follow them, interact with them, and treat them like gold.

A third way is to interview and associate with influencers in the 1 percent for columns, videos, webinars, and more and then borrow their audience, since their audience learns more about you.

And more, but that's probably enough for an answer today.

The real key for all of us is that it is very doable to break down influence and understand how it is created and whether it lasts or dissipates. The question for us is what we do about it, which is something I have talked about in my other books (*Pre-Commerce, Storytizing,* and *Crafting Persuasion*).

LEADERSHIP INSIGHT

Great Leaders Give You the Gift of Trust

I remember when I reported to Jean-Jacques Bienaime, who was senior vice president of marketing for Rhône-Poulenc Rorer and is now chairman and CEO of BioMarin. I walked in to see JJ and explained what we recommended and how much it would cost. He listened to me and said, "Ok, sounds good. Let's do it."

His clarity and trust in me made me work twice as hard to ensure I deserved the gift of trust he gave me.

I know everyone didn't get an ok every time, but he had a way of showing his support that let you know he understood your ask and had your back. Now it was on me and my team to make it real.

When a leader unlocks another leader, they also unlock a powerful form of accountability.

Ask yourself if you are doing that with your team.

CHAPTER 39

THE TIME VALUE OF AN IDEA

"Creativity is thinking up new things.
Innovation is doing new things."
— Theodore Levitt

It always seems like anyone who gambles wins big, yet most actually lose their money.

It's the same with startups and new ideas. We hear about the victories but seldom the defeats.

If you are a leader, a member of your team may approach you with a new idea for a product, a new service, a new practice, or even a new firm to create. You will assess its value and make a decision.

I'll assume you have done great research, have resources, and are smart. Now, despite all these advantages, why do so many ideas still fail? Seems odd, right?

Not really, if we think of the time value of an idea.

What is most important is the ability to understand when a new idea has the ability to scale across multiple clients or within your company and when it is too early or late.

What is equally important is understanding how the marketplace will evolve over the next three to five years, so that you are sailing with the wind instead of going against it.

Here is an example from the healthcare industry:

When researchers developed the first human genome map, everyone imagined how the world would change. Then, the race started to sequence our genes. Again, everyone imagined great success, yet not much occurred.

Guess who is making the money?

It is the entrepreneurs who imagined how to apply this knowledge in new ways. Companies like ancestry.com, 23andMe, Helix, and others make sense of genetic data in ways that are helpful to us. Then, there are pharmaceutical and biotechnology companies who develop new gene therapy treatments.

It is often the entrepreneur who figures out how to "apply knowledge" that wins.

Now, why do so many great ideas that apply knowledge in new ways still fail?

There are a range of reasons, but I would say courage is the main one.

It is easy to develop a new platform, champion it, speak about it, and do pilots with companies. It is difficult and a bit scary to go for it and see if you can scale your idea across dozens, then hundreds and thousands of companies. That means you might fail. You may run out of resources. You may have to completely change your platform to succeed. You basically must go all in and align with your audience.

It is this path in the road that separates creative thinking from innovation.

In your network, think of all the startups you know who have a great idea, love what they have built, and talk about who they are conducting pilots with to test their ideas. They are always testing.

How many of them tell you how they are scaling worldwide with these same companies?

How many of them discuss how their revenue per employee is rapidly increasing?

How many of them articulate the specific business problems they are solving?

Too often, we hear the opposite. We hear about how much money they have raised and what they will raise next. We hear about who is investing in their company. We hear about things that don't relate to building scalable innovation.

Meanwhile, your competitors are thinking of similar ideas. And here is a big "aha" for many creators:

If you think your idea is unique, you are wrong. Somewhere on this earth, someone else is thinking of the same thing at the same time. So, as you consider your next steps, the clock is ticking.

Your idea has a time value on it and an expiration date.

My experience has shown me that many creative ideas have died a slow death due to the lack of their founder's courage to take a chance and scale their idea.

The ones that do are the ones we remember. And the ones that fail to do so often learn enough to be successful the next time around.

Whether you have an idea for a new product, service, practice, or firm, think through how you will apply knowledge and how it will scale and have the courage of your convictions to see it through.

It is an exhausting, inspiring, and educational process to go through.

It is why we describe some of our friends as serial entrepreneurs. They deserve the moniker.

CHAPTER 40

THE UNTAPPED VALUE OF SEARCH

"The only thing Google has failed to do, so far, is fail."

—John Battelle

It's funny how we stop thinking when we believe we have an answer.

Search engine optimization is a great example.

Google represents nearly one-third of online ad revenue worldwide (29 percent actually), so it is safe to say the advertising world understands the relevance of Google.

Collectively, we all conduct about two trillion searches per year, so it is also safe to say that the average person knows the value of Google.

And yet it remains one of the most underleveraged media platforms on earth. Why?

Part of the reason is we don't make it easy enough for our partners to fully understand what is possible. Therefore, it is often useful to share our insights. Over time, what we are really doing is teaching.

As an example, let's focus on five key ideas or insights related to Google.

#1 – Use a new Venn diagram. We know that our desire to learn (organic search) generates 53.3 percent of global web traffic and 93 percent of consumers in the US use local search to find businesses. So, what if we analyze search and compare it to our campaigns? We will find that different influencers, topics, channels, and keywords matter versus the ones we are currently using to reach customers today. Think of it like a Venn diagram. You have your existing campaign and believe you know who the right influencers, channels, content, and words are. And then you have what Google tells us based on the actions of those same customers. It is worth rethinking our analytics approach.

#2 – Understand how a reputation is built over decades. If we use the Wayback Machine and develop our own analytic processes, we can see how a reputation is built worldwide over decades by looking at websites, media channels, and the story that has evolved over time. We often review a reputation based on what is in the news today (important), but we spend less time understanding the dynamics that have created this same reputation over a decade or two or three. This is a real opportunity for communicators.

#3 – See how audio search differs from written search. Worldwide, more than 50 percent of search is now via voice. In the US, that number is about 40 percent of search. Our desire for audio search is more important, with 71 percent of us preferring to give a voice versus written query. This is a transformative shift in how we use language to search, which impacts SEO and SEM and gives us a different window into how people think. This is a very rich area for analytics to shine as we learn the differences and relevant insights from voice search.

#4 – Dig in and see how bias is impacting search results. Google is dominant, but there are still about sixteen search engines in the world that have some level of traction. If we look at how these search engines report on the same news, it is striking how different the same story is, depending on where you live and what language you prefer. The most glaring example today relates to the Ukraine/Russia war and how Yandex (Russia-based search engine) indexes content on the war (Russia is evidently doing amazing) and how Google shows results on the war (some information is not shown due to its filters).

When two trillion searches are being conducted each year, I will make the argument that understanding why certain information is indexed and featured versus information that is suppressed and blocked matters. It is worthy of a continual discussion.

#5 – Create a new search media relations role. And this leads to the big opportunity for communicators and marketers. In my view, larger teams should include a search media relations professional who can gather intelligence to shape campaigns, examine how a brand or company's reputation is being shaped, understand and stay ahead of how keywords are evolving, and take these learnings to conduct outreach to new influencers, rethink the current media plan, and recalibrate the SEO strategy.

And that's just what is worth sharing in a quick update.

Google and search engines overall are the digital id of our world. Not identity, but the id, as in Freud's work.

It's a window into how we really feel about what is happening day-to-day and what matters to us.

CHAPTER 41

WHY GREAT STORYTELLERS OFTEN BECOME LEADERS

"The most powerful person in the world is the storyteller. The storyteller sets the vision, values and agenda of an entire generation that is to come."

—*Steve Jobs*

Ideas and insights drive the consulting business.

If they remain in our heads, their value is either never realized or depreciates every day until they become worthless.

It is our ability to communicate, to tell a story, that allows an *insight* to evolve into an *idea* that can lead to a campaign that makes a difference.

Choosing to learn how to tell a story is one we often avoid.

We may be intimidated to speak in public.

We may not want to lead a meeting, thinking this is for other people to do.

We may not share our point of view in writing since we don't know if others will like it.

We have a list of reasons in our heads as to why we don't learn how to present our ideas with the passion and intellect that resides in our heads right now.

Why?

Warren Buffett, one of the most successful investors in the history of the world, said that the only certificate on his wall is from the Dale Carnegie Institute, where he learned to overcome his fears of public speaking. Without that ability, he would be just another investor.

When we learn to calm our anxiety about presenting our ideas, our ability to share, learn, and iterate goes up exponentially.

It's why leaders are generally good at articulating concepts and telling stories. They made a commitment in their careers to figure out how to do it, accept the occasional rejection of their ideas, and power on.

Your insights and ideas deserve their time in the spotlight. Don't hold back.

If you learn to write in a public forum, you can express your ideas and influence those who follow you.

If you learn to present, you can lead a room as you tell a compelling story.

If you can do both, you will probably lead a business of some type in the future.

Your ideas are waiting. Don't let them down.

CHAPTER 42

HOW TO DESCRIBE A NEW MODEL

"Innovation is taking two things that exist and putting them together in a new way."

— *Tom Freston*

When we look closely at the most successful business models, we usually have the same observation: "That's pretty simple. Why didn't someone else think of that?"

All the technologies needed to create the iPhone already existed, but Steve Jobs and Jony Ive surprised us with device after device because of their ability to package and design solutions we soon realized we needed.

VRBO—Just renting out your property in new ways

Uber—Taxi cabs, now using personal cars with mapping software

Peloton—A more fun way to exercise with virtual partners

The list goes on.

So how do we describe a new model that we have developed? One that we are sure the world needs.

Simple, or at least the end result is simple. The process takes effort.

Below is the process to go through to describe a new model. If you can do this, you are on your way.

#1 – Define the unmet need. What is the unmet need in the market you are addressing? When you explain it, you should see heads nod, since it is clear this is a pain point.

#2 – Visualize the solution in the most simplistic way. Describe your solution so your client can leave the meeting, walk down the hall, and explain it to their boss in thirty to sixty seconds, and they get it.

#3 – Provide use cases for your first five to ten uses. You have provided a use case that is perfect for their situation, so they can imagine, with you, how the model will work.

#4 – Provide thought leadership/explanations to help your clients explain the model internally. You have additional content that provides further detail to explain how the model works.

Each of these steps is difficult, because each one requires precise thinking that opens minds and illustrates how simple your solution is.

Now, equally important is how you destroy the potential of a model from the perspective of a client.

#1 – Focus on your model and vaguely address the unmet need. If I can't determine the exact problem to fix, I am not moving forward.

#2 – Revel in your technology awesomeness. It sounds amazing, but I can't buy "smart," I need to buy the "solution" to my problem.

#3 – Provide one hundred cases or none. It's overwhelming, so I shut down. Don't have time to weed through a library.

#4 – Inundate the client with an answer for everything. Shows you don't know me, so you are accounting for every scenario. Just focus on my needs.

Here are examples from our world:

Unmet need – We don't know how physicians, nurses, patients, media, payors, and other influencers interact online and influence each other, if they do at all.

Visualize the solution – Audience Architecture shows us how each person interacts across digital media channels. We show who they follow, who they respect, and what content they engage in, and then we can visualize this audience ecosystem for you.

Use case – Let's figure out how people with a rare disease interact in the US over the last year.

Thought leadership – Create posts on what Audience Architecture is, the importance of using the right data sources, why understanding how an audience interacts is more important than traditional media techniques, how to measure it, and more.

We also know that few people want to go deep on the data science, understand every data source, or go deep on the specifics of each algorithm. Ninety-nine percent of leaders want to understand that one sentence describing the idea and then hear more about how it could work for them (the use case). In fact, if we share too much on that, it turns off people, at least initially.

Our focus is basic.

The unmet need, the simple description, the relevant use case, and thought leadership that explains it all.

Looks easy when done well. Worth the effort.

I have personally seen this work hundreds of times. I have also witnessed how complexity can kill an idea just in how it is presented. Stay simple, and you'll be pleased with the results.

LEADERSHIP INSIGHT

Be Careful with How You Handle Awards

I was in sixth grade, and our team, the Eagles, had just won our town's Little League "World Series." Soon, we walked on stage at the Millburn Chanticler to accept our trophies. When I got home, I said to my dad, "I can't believe I won this trophy," like you might expect an eleven-year-old to say.

My dad got kind of mad at me and said, "Bobby, you didn't win this trophy. Your team did. Don't ever say that you won when it is always the team."

He was right. I knew he was right. I felt bad in the moment, but my dad taught me yet another lifelong lesson I am so glad I learned.

Anytime you get an award, even for individual achievement, just remember it never is just for you. Share the wealth.

FINANCIAL

CHAPTER 43

A RISING TIDE LIFTS ALL BOATS

WHY INCENTIVES MATTER

"Show me the incentive and I will show you the outcome."

— Charlie Munger

When we create an incentive, we should ask a simple question:

Will this incentive lead to actions that will create value for the long term?

If the incentive inspires us to create new value that can help all of us, we are on the right track.

Incentives literally "encourage" us to try new things and engage in behavior that goes above and beyond the norm.

We cover the "norm" via salary, bonus, and promotions. The norm includes managing our portfolio of business and bringing in new team members or clients. This is the normal flow of a business like ours.

Incentives guide us to go "above the norm."

We might grow the revenue of a practice beyond what was forecasted. Or create new models that open new doors with clients. Or expand our work with a client based on phenomenal results and service. Or we figure out a way to become more efficient financially.

Rewarding exceptional results leads to long-term value that is meaningful to all of us.

Transactional incentives lead to, you guessed it, transactional behavior. We think more about ourselves and how we win versus how our firm will do.

We are here to build the industry's leading practices and the offerings that go with it.

Think of it this way. Incentives should always align with those moments when we are especially proud of what we are accomplishing.

Our practice just experienced 20 percent growth year to year! Wow!

Our new media models just led to ten new client assignments! More Wow!

Our organic growth is the strongest in the firm and is setting the standard for all. Even More Wow!

It is important for us not to let incentives become a normal expectation. Normal is good. It can pay for a strong salary and a normal bonus.

Incentives are reserved for results that propel a firm forward. And when we do this, the assistant account executive wins as much as the senior vice president in terms of new assignments, faster career development, and ultimately, more compensation as we all rise.

A rising tide lifts all boats.

CHAPTER 44

THE ART OF BUDGETING AND FORECASTING

KEY LEARNINGS

"The most reliable way to forecast the future is to try to understand the present."

—John Naisbitt

BUDGET VERSUS FORECAST

Our budget is our operational plan. Our forecast reflects our view of the future. We need both to be well done to guide us as we build our firm.

The operational plan allocates funds to match up with our client fee income plan that we are confident we can hit. This ensures that our spending matches our incoming fee. It is like keeping a balanced check book.

Our forecast helps us see where we are going next. It tells us what we could do in terms of organic growth and new business. Our pipeline shows how the marketplace views us in terms of size/shape/type of client. It also shows the commitment we have to build our respective practices.

In general, if a pipeline's value is 50 percent of the total value of the expected annual fee income, we have a healthy pipeline, since not everything will come in as expected. For example, if a practice expects $10MM in fee income, a healthy pipeline is valued at $5MM.

OUR SHADOW FORECAST

A shadow forecast reflects our view of what we are capable of reaching each year. We look at all forms of growth and assume we can reach a stretch goal. This forecast doesn't impact our operational plan unless it becomes real, then it allows us to make agile decisions since we have already anticipated this growth via this more aggressive scenario plan.

A typical stretch goal is at least 10 percent more than the operational plan. In some years, it may be more, and it can differ by practice. There are not any scenarios where we don't have a stretch goal, unless we think we are losing ground in the market.

In this same scenario, if we have a budget of $10MM in annual fee income, our stretch goal might be $11MM.

We do this for a simple reason. When we continually pursue growth, we identify new opportunities faster, create more options for career growth for our team, and have a better chance of building a stronger bonus pool. We also ensure that we end the year with more momentum, so that we go strong into the next fiscal year.

HOW WE VALUE OUR PIPELINE

Our pipeline is valuable to us for three key reasons:

Plan our future—If we add in all potential organic growth opportunities and all potential clients, we know how we expect to grow. It's important to list all we know and not just add in when we are sure. We discount these opportunities at 25 percent, which means we are aware of the opportunities, but they do not influence our value. Perhaps the biggest value is we are shaping our future rather than reacting to what is incoming alone.

Compete to win—We will always have opportunities where we are competing. If we are one of three or more firms, we are still at 25 percent. If we believe we are now in the top two, we are now at 50 percent, and this is included in our value. If the client is near a decision and it's highly likely we will win, it goes to 75 percent.

Note: The best firms win close to 50 percent of all competitive pitches.

No-pitch opportunities—This is organic growth and no-pitch opportunities for new business, often based on our network and reputations. If we believe the assignment will come in, but it may take some time, we put this at 50 percent. If we believe we are in great shape and just need to complete the proposal/SOW, we put this at 75 percent.

Note 1: Over time, the underlying growth of our firm should include at least 10 percent organic growth and at least 5 percent no-pitch opportunities. If we use the $10MM example, we will go into the next year and plan for $1MM in organic growth and $500k in no-pitch opportunities, in addition to new business.

Note 2: Our client retention rate greatly impacts our forecast each year. Our goal is to be 90 percent or better at retaining clients and the same level of revenue each year. As you can see, if we lose 10 percent, we then need to grow 10 percent in organic and 10 percent in new business to achieve a 10 percent overall growth rate. Hence, the better retention we have, the healthier we are.

Note 3: Our client teams are SO important. The splendid work we do to wow clients and exceed their expectations leads to strong retention and strong organic growth. This is a key part of building a great firm.

Overall, it is important that we are candid about where we stand on each opportunity. If we are too conservative or too aggressive, our forecasting will be off. Be courageous and candid and have fun creating a business portfolio we enjoy working on every day.

CHAPTER 45

HOW A FORECAST CAN BECOME YOUR COMPASS

"Weather forecast for tonight: dark."

— *George Carlin*

A forecast is an estimate of future events. It is our best guess. And it is the equivalent of a compass that guides us in the right direction.

George Carlin, who was an irreverent comedian known for lambasting societal norms, makes a point here that we want to avoid.

A forecast is not an accurate assessment of today's business. Too many leaders avoid making a real diagnosis of their business, so they build a plan based on what they are sure will happen and call that a forecast.

That's not a forecast. That's a budget and a plan.

So, what is a forecast? And how can it guide us?

A compass has the answers. This device is designed for location, navigation, and direction. It is built to detect and respond to signals (magnetism) from our earth. And it is fairly accurate!

Here's our version for building our firms:

Location—A compass tells us where we are right now. In our world, we center our forecast on the following metrics that serve as "coordinates."

Client retention—How many clients and how much of our revenue in this year will continue with us the following year? We normally shoot for 90 percent or better.

Organic growth—Our clients vote on our work by giving us more opportunities to provide value, similar to how internal client teams take on more responsibility when their bosses believe in their work. In consulting, we look for 10-20 percent organic growth, with 20 percent being the more frequent standard.

Size of clients—The size of our clients tells us where we are having success in the market. We could be attracting clients in the Series A to IPO range or Fortune 500 companies. The clues are in the analysis.

Team productivity—How many billable hours do our team members bill each year, and what is the revenue per team member per year? Generally, we look to see how close a fully billable team member gets to 1,800 total hours for the year. The revenue per team member lets us see if our pricing is on target via further analysis.

Navigation—Now that we know what the current state looks like, our next set of questions relates to where we will go next. This includes areas such as:

Practice areas—We ask which practices are showing the most potential and estimate how they can grow in the following year(s). This can include industries such as healthcare or financial, for example. We may be doing $5MM in an industry today, but we can see we have the momentum to get to $8MM. But how do we know this?

Pipeline—Our pipeline is the best navigation device we will ever have, which is why it is so important to build it accurately. In general, you want a pipeline that is 50 percent of your total revenue for the year. Why? Because you will only win 25-50 percent of that total, and you have to make up for a 10 percent loss of business before you can get to positive growth for the next year. Being accurate in updating your pipeline and discounting value properly are keys to success.

Win rate–How often do you win in new business? How does your win rate differ by type of opportunity (RFP versus no competition)? How often do you receive organic growth opportunities? Understanding the nuances of your win rate helps you accurately portray the value of your pipeline. Just loading in a bunch of stuff with big numbers is fairly useless.

Team size/span–Now, we think of how and why our teams need to grow. What skills are missing or need to be strengthened? Where do we need new team members due to the higher volume of work? And who in our current team has the ability to manage a larger team? This exercise, which is often skipped, is absolutely critical to success. Think of this "talent pipeline" as being the equivalent of a growth pipeline.

Office size–Here, we answer two simple questions: Where are our clients, current and future, located? Where does the talent live to serve these clients? They are often in the same place, of course, so we actively forecast how large our New York City office should become versus our Chicago office based on the answers to these two questions.

Direction–Now we get to the really fun part. Where do we go next? Here is where we can either stretch ourselves to build our firm or avoid the conversation and just kind of wing it. If we don't wing it, here is what we recommend:

Practices–Which industries can we serve better?

New areas–Are we ready to serve an entirely new industry?

New geographies–Where do we need to build an office/presence to attract the clients we desire?

New leaders – What type of leaders can join us who will provide new networks of clients, talent, and ideas?

New offerings – What are the new offerings that will provide additional value to our clients and improve our level of competitiveness?

If we answer these questions to the best of our ability, we are on the path to building a forecast that will impact the following areas of our firm:

Financial – We can judge how we are doing versus our forecast. We then update our forecast every three months, keeping the original as a guide, but adjusting to reality as we go forward.

Human Resources – We understand key areas of career development for our team and the recruitment of talent.

Investment – We know what type of people and offerings we are looking for to join us, so we can become the best in our business.

This is what we think of in a forecast. A more holistic approach where the numbers serve as a guide, and we build our own compass to keep telling us how we are doing, just like a compass does as we travel.

Once you build a plan that can keep getting smarter as you evolve as a firm, you realize you can't live without it. It's like walking without knowing what direction you are going in and hoping you do ok.

Leaders build compasses. Leaders play chess. And leaders are determined to keep evolving their forecast based on reality versus holding on to last year's ideas.

LEADERSHIP INSIGHT

Humor Is a Business Skill

When I was in sales, Charlie Rhyne was our regional director for the southeast region, which, in my view of the world, was the most important person I could imagine meeting.

Charlie was a powerful leader who all respected, so I studied him whenever possible. And what I noticed is how he used humor so skillfully.

Charlie knew how to tell a joke, often based on the moment, which would release the tension in the room. He didn't tell long stories. Rather, he played off the tension he felt in a way that dissipated it.

I remember when we were having an all-hands meeting with the president of CIBA-GEIGY and other top brass in Atlanta, where Charlie was based. It was an important moment, perhaps a bit too formal for most of us, and as Charlie grabbed the microphone, it made a rather distinctive sound. Charlie paused, looked at us, said, "Excuse me," paused again, and the entire place burst into laughter.

It sounds silly, but it lightened up the room, and we had a great meeting as Charlie proceeded to introduce the president.

CHAPTER 46

THE MOST IMPORTANT FINANCIAL METRICS FOR AN ACCOUNT LEADER

"In business, the idea of measuring what you are doing, picking the measurements that count like customer satisfaction and performance...you thrive on that."

—*Bill Gates*

Picking the measurements that count. That is profound advice from Bill Gates.

We have lots of metrics for account team leaders—billability, revenue per employee, satisfaction scores, and more. But what really matters?

What matters is measuring the actions and outcomes directly related to building a successful and sustainable team. The other metrics may be interesting, but are not nearly as important. In fact, they can be distracting.

Here are the top seven metrics for a successful account leader:

Client retention—If you are doing a wonderful job for your client, they will continue with you the following year. We know things happen. Client leads leave their companies, a company is acquired, or a product or service is discontinued. So, we assume that a 90 percent retention rate year to year is healthy. This means, of course, that you need to add in 10 percent growth to break-even the following year.

Metric – *"My goal is to ensure >90 percent of our current business returns the following year."*

Organic growth – Clients vote with their pocketbook and their network. If clients love our work, they think of new ways to collaborate with us (organic growth) and/or they introduce us to new people in their network or participate with us in thought leadership that expands both of our networks. Strong organic growth is generally in the 10-20 percent level on an annual basis, depending on the size of your clients and their ability to grow together.

Metric – *"My goal is to ensure we have organic growth of 10-20 percent each year."*

Team structure and +4 – If you will scale well and continue to provide high-quality work, then you will be involved in two important actions. You will build a +4 of direct reports that are each as good as you or better in key areas. Each of your +4's will, in turn, build out their team from the entry level team members to individuals who may replace them someday.

Metric – *"My goal is to ensure I improve my +4 (could be starting with a +1) and improve the direct report structure of my reports."*

New business growth – If you are engaged in thought leadership in some form and have a healthy relationship with your clients, you will enjoy new business opportunities. In addition, you either know people in your industry or can get to know them over time. Create your own network of people you want to work with. It's likely they will want to, as well. This also represents 10-20 percent of annual growth.

Metric – *"My goal is to ensure I identify and succeed in bringing in new opportunities that represent 10-20 percent of revenue each year."*

Industry and offering expertise – You build a plan that identifies the companies that are complementary to your current client base and team's expertise so that your future clients keep improving your overall acumen and your current clients feel this advantage. You also review your offering with the intent of introducing new skills that can add value to your client.

Metric – *"My goal is to bring in one to two new clients from this ecosystem and offer one to two new skills to my client via our offering."*

Client satisfaction and your plan – You speak with your team weekly on how you are providing the best service/value to your clients. Your goal is to secure a 4.5 out of 5 on the client satisfaction survey your firm conducts annually. And you and your team know what you are specifically working on to achieve your goals.

Metric – *"My goal is for us to achieve a 4.5 satisfaction ranking and work on one to two new areas this year to ensure we improve our team's capabilities and acumen."*

Learning and partnering – You look at yourself and your team and ensure that everyone has a learning plan, even if informal. You also look within your firm to identify where you can partner.

Metric – *"My goal is to ensure each team member knows their learning plan and completes it, and we identify at least one partner where we can learn what they do and introduce this service/product to our clients."*

CHAPTER 47

WHAT DO INVESTORS CARE ABOUT?

"There's no shortage of remarkable ideas, what's missing is the will to execute them."

—*Seth Godin*

There often comes a time in a firm's life when you consider seeking an investment.

You know your business inside and out because you work every day to solve client problems and create new opportunities. Now, you are seeking a cash infusion.

Remember that investors do the same. They look at hundreds of companies to figure out which ones have real upside. They are just as good as you are, and their skill is analysis…of you.

I've been fortunate to be an adviser for several private equity firms over the years to provide my industry perspective. In turn, I feel like I have picked up a second MBA just by listening to what they care about.

I would never say there is such a thing as "the list" you just need to follow. Rather, I can share what is common across most situations I have had a chance to participate in.

Imagine being on the other side of the table as an investor. You are looking at your firm and asking the following questions:

- **Leadership team** – How deep is your current leadership team?

- How strong is your next generation of leaders?
- Where is it important that you improve?

- **Integration** – Show the integration of your services across clients year to year.
  - Assume 50-60 percent of clients use two to three different services to be competitive.

- **Client excellence** – How do you measure?
  - How do you improve?

- **Client portfolio** – How are you growing clients year to year, and how is this changing your portfolio?
  - What new types of clients/industries are we shifting towards? What type of clients are inside these sectors? Right ones? Why?
  - Is your platform capable of scaling multiple practices?

- **Products and services** – How does your innovation translate into revenue?
  - What is the actual revenue per year for your lead products and services?
  - What is the "X" factor that gets you in the door? How many X factors do you have?

- **Organic growth** – What is your plan, how organized is it, and how dependable is your growth?
  - Show at least 10 percent growth YTY via organic growth (this is after making up for client loss).
  - How do you measure client excellence? Why are you better at it than most firms?

- **Firm integration** – Is everyone benefiting from how you are scaling and focusing on their growth?
  - If any team or firm is not on board, why are they part of the exit? Rationale?
  - What operational inefficiencies do you have, and why do you have them?

- **Size of pipeline**—Is your pipeline equal to 50 percent of your FY revenue forecast?
    - How do you source your pipeline, and how does this relate to your win percentage?
    - How strong is your market positioning via thought leadership, awards, and other leader recognition?
- **Type of "wins"**—How many are no pitch? How many have an "unfair advantage"?
    - Total win percentage should be 50 percent or greater when all types of opportunities are factored in.
- **Financial**—What is the profitability by client?
    - How do you build your teams using capacity analysis?
    - Are you excellent at scaling teams, or are you winging it?
- **Client size**—How many clients over $1MM? $3MM? $5MM? $10MM?
    - Show clear path towards larger clients.
    - What is the potential for all clients versus current revenue?
    - What does that "gap" look like, and what is your plan?

The question for you, as a leader, is how well you can answer these questions.

It takes many years to answer these questions with affirmative answers.

Your decision as a leader is quite simple.

Do you want to build a firm that has the ability to continually grow? We call it a scalable firm.

Or do you prefer to have a well-run firm that is stable and predictable? We call it a lifestyle firm.

Either decision is yours, no one else's.

Just remember that it takes years to show up strong. You can't decide one day to try harder next year and be ready. For those of us who look at firms from a thirty-thousand-foot view, we can see the difference with relative ease.

My view is there is a more important reason why you may choose to build a scalable firm.

You will build careers for your team members faster and with more upside for each of them. You will work in a more dynamic environment. And you may find that giving up control to other leaders is actually more fun than tightly controlling every decision along the way.

Again, your call. Just remember what will define you in the eyes of an investor if that time ever arrives for you.

CHAPTER 48

WHAT DOES UTILIZATION MEAN?

"The act of measurement changes both the event and the observer."

—Peter Drucker

Service firms screw this up continually. The question is why?

The short answer is we often make things way too complicated, organizationally, as we try to control outcomes.

When we place too much emphasis on percentages and weekly numbers and hyperventilate over short-term dips in performance, we end up changing the event and the observer, as Peter Drucker points out.

The members of our firm dislike the process, it feels very impersonal, and it can instill fear, one of the worst emotions to have in the hallways of any service firm.

Like any model, it is important to strip it apart and ask what we are really trying to do.

We want to know if each team member is as productive as they can be during the year.

We want to know if we are building the most effective team, if our pricing is accurate to our workflow, and as a result, are we building profitable growth?

We want to see if our teams are structured optimally and how to improve.

But think of how we typically address this situation.

We send reminders out weekly to "get your time in the system," or we take the other approach and say, "We don't input time; we don't believe in it."

We occasionally threaten to shut down email if time is not in.

We judge people's contributions based on their percentage of billability on a week or month of work, which could be impacted by how leaders allocate business versus how strong a team member is.

How much more impersonal can you get?

Great models are always simple. A degree in rocket science is not required.

What follows is what we need to do to understand if we are building a firm that will increase or maintain its profitability as we grow.

EVERY TEAM MEMBER KNOWS THEIR NUMBER OF BILLABLE HOURS FOR THE YEAR

#1 – Measure billable hours for the year. The most important step is to set an annual target for billable hours by position, e.g., 1500 for a vice president versus 1600 for an account supervisor. By doing this, you do not become distracted by weekly billable percentages, PTO's impact, or other factors. Each team member either is on track to hitting their numbers for the year, or they are not.

You know what each person at each title should bill for the year. You have rolled this number into your forecast.

ONLY MEASURE WHAT IS BILLED TO THE CLIENT

#2 – Billable hours means hours *actually* billed. Take the time to understand where you have overage, so you can see how many billable hours are actually billed. Only count these hours towards the annual total. You will usually be running one to two months behind here, but once you get started, you will have a rolling average.

You will see more clearly where some team members are billing every hour they work. Others are having 20-30 percent of their time not making it to a bill. This could be due to the quality of their work, or it may be that a leader isn't accurately planning. It's quite often the latter, FYI.

ANNUAL REVENUE UNCOVERS OUR ISSUES

#3 – Multiply billable hours by the hourly rate to understand revenue per employee. If you work 200 hours for one client at $300 per hour, this equals $60,000.00. If you work another 200 hours for $200 per hour, that is $40,000.00. Same person, but dramatically different results. Work with this reality. At the end of the year, you will be able to see that person ABC billed 1200 hours times a mixed rate of $250 or $300,000.00 for the year. Use absolute numbers with real billing rates.

We often undervalue our time. Why? If we need to spend time to build a new relationship or practice, then we are investing in our future. But, if this is normal staffing, we are avoiding a conversation about why we are discounting our work or perhaps not building the team that matches the work.

NEVER HIDE BEHIND A FIXED RATE

#4 – Always use actual billable hourly rates internally, even if you provide a fixed rate. We now want to understand how we are optimizing each person's time. In this same scenario, we know that the hourly rate for this team member is $300 per hour, so for 1200 hours, they should bill $360,000.00. However, they billed $300,000.00 in this scenario, which means we are choosing to give a $60,000.00 discount to select clients over the year based on our pricing model.

Own it.

KNOW YOUR TRUE INVESTMENT

#5 – Measure per client based on this model. Some of our team works 100 percent for a client, while others may work 20 percent. Since we are looking at absolute numbers, we simply do the math and figure out how we are doing. In doing this, we may find we are asking a senior vice president, who bills at $400 per hour, to work 1,000 hours per year on an account where we can only charge $250 per hour. So, we are giving up $150 per hour in opportunity cost each year, which is equal to $150,000.00. Again, this is a discount we are actively choosing to give.

You will find that we are often "losing" money on senior leaders when this situation occurs. This is a separate discussion on how we build total value (billable hours, organic growth, new business) as we grow in our careers.

KNOW YOUR OPPORTUNITY COST AND HOW TO IMPROVE

#6 – Clarify if you are making an investment or simply overservicing. The first question to answer is how much we are discounting to our clients by how we price, as outlined in #4. This is our first discount, if we are doing so. The second is how much we are working but not charging in terms of hours. If a client relationship is healthy and the account is profitable, 10 percent is a normal "overage," if any is needed at all. But let's use an example where we underbill and have an overage that is normal. In this scenario, we find that our team (#4) is discounting $150,000.00 by how we price our time, and in this account (let's say it's $1MM in fee per year), we also have an overage of 10 percent or $100,000.00. So, we are consciously discounting a total of $250,000.00 in potential fee income to keep and service a $1MM account.

The good news is that if we stick to absolute numbers and show ourselves reality, we find it is quite easy to gradually improve our profit margin. Be sure to avoid the London fog approach. When people game time, they will hide behind percentages and fixed hourly rates, distort weekly percentages based on how they use non-billable time, and find other ways to pump up their percentages.

It is my view that when client leaders understand the reality of the numbers for their team, they will incrementally improve their position, which is healthy for our team and client and improves our bonus pool over time.

As you think about how to do this, ask yourself this question:

Do I manage by fear (get your time in or else)? Do I manage by ignorance (we don't need to know our billable time; we don't do that)? Or do I manage via math (let's be logical and see how we improve as a team)?

One of these three builds profitable growth that scales well. Wondering which one?

An easy choice.

TALENT

CHAPTER 49

DEALING WITH THE "FEARS" OF CONSULTING

"Have no fear of perfection—you'll never reach it."
—*Salvador Dali*

Part of being human is dealing with fear. It's not unique or bad. It just is.

We need to look no further than Maslow's hierarchy of needs to understand how it relates to consulting.

Maslow's pyramid has five levels. In each level, we can be well-balanced, or we may have elements of fear that drive us. That is totally normal.

Let's explore each one and relate it to what we do during the workday. Here we go, from the bottom up:

Physiological Needs (food and clothing)—Our most basic need is ensuring we have food and clothing.

Safety—We are concerned about job security, health, and resources for living day to day.

Love and Belonging—We desire friendship, a sense of connection.

Esteem—Confidence in ourselves, respect, and recognition.

Self-Actualization—Desire to become the most one can be.

If this is what is driving all of us throughout our lives, let's look at some of the most basic "fears" we deal with to become the best consultants.

The fear of failure – We often say that our worst moment is when a client says, "I don't like your work." To this day, it leaves a pit in the stomach of anyone in this business who cares. We live to exceed expectations, so when we don't, we feel momentarily like a failure. It's driven by our desire to connect and our own esteem.

The fear of speaking – We are often too worried about being perfect, so we limit our exposure to failing. In reality, the more often we speak, the more we practice unlocking our talent. Love and Belonging and Esteem are fighting with Self-Actualization. We kind of know we should practice more, but what if we don't do well? It's this type of "noise" that we need to help diminish, so we can all be the best we can be over time.

The fear of being unrecognized for our talents – We want to end our careers knowing we were able to become the best consultant we are capable of becoming, whatever that may be. We don't want any barriers in the way. And we sure don't want to be ignored.

So, what do great firms do?

We build a culture that is real. It shows respect and recognition for all employees. It builds a sense of connection among all levels. And it focuses on "unlocking" each person, since Self-Actualization is a pretty cool level to operate at. The firm is all about getting to the fifth level over time. No short cuts, but a clear commitment.

We stay centered in the reality that each person has a different version of what *security* means to them. It is often related to where a person is in their life. It could be personal (more money can lead to a better apartment) or career development (can I be promoted multiple times at this firm) to am I learning (new skills) to do the work I like (am I excited to do my best every day). We each have our own unique mix.

We embrace a style that encourages team members to learn how to present, how to run a meeting, and how to allow their personality and expertise to shine together. We know a great firm works hard and serves as a training ground for the future.

I've learned that if we stay centered on what drives us, we can often figure ourselves out far faster.

There is a tendency for us to want things, say that we would do more "if only this happened," or complain about our situation to a friend.

Understanding what drives us is a psychological mirror. It helps us stay self-aware and recalibrate ourselves.

In our firm, we use the symbol of a lock and key for this very reason. Our goal is to unlock each individual's capabilities. You know it when it's happening, and you know it when it's not.

None of us will ever be perfect, but why would we want to be? It's our differences all working together that result in the best ideas, the best campaigns, and the best firms. Our mission is to help all of us make this journey simpler and fun.

LEADERSHIP INSIGHT

Imagine Your Legacy Now

It may seem odd to think of how people will remember you decades from now, but it is never too early to think like this.

What will you be remembered for?

Professionally? Personally? By your closest friends?

What really matters?

Push yourself to dream about what you can do. After all, we only live once, and it is up to us to make the most of our time.

Most importantly, whatever you decide, have fun getting there. Enjoy life every day you have and help others do the same.

And take a moment when you are on an airplane or waiting in the terminal for your next flight to ask yourself, how am I making a difference?

CHAPTER 50

HOW TO NAVIGATE THE WORKPLACE

"A ship that sails without a compass will get lost at sea."

—*Matshona Dhliwayo*

A ship's captain shares many of the same traits with a managing partner building the next great consulting firm.

A captain must plan, direct, and plot the path and position of their ship, so they can travel across the sea. Ahead of them are unknown currents, dangerous storms, and, of course, blue skies and calm water.

It is the ability to continually prepare for the journey while it is occurring that sets apart the leaders from the followers.

In the world of consulting, the captains navigate what's important in society and continue to plan, direct, and plot the path and position of the firm, while absorbing knowledge and new skills that will help in the journey.

Meanwhile, waves hit the ship, and storms brew in the distance. Change is ahead.

Captains don't overreact. They plan for change. If they don't, the change may send them off in a direction that may lead to an unpredictable situation.

In our world, each wave or storm can have a silver lining, and it's important we look for it.

What learning can we take in from each change, integrate into our journey, and become stronger?

You see, the followers don't think like this. They overreact to every headline. They are worried that if they don't change immediately, everyone will leave. They are filled with anxiety. They see one firm do something and think they must do it.

They stopped thinking about how to navigate their own ship.

And a rudderless ship won't end up in a good place.

Recently, we had quite a storm we refer to as the Covid-19 era.

Here's how captains reacted to this storm:

We think of what we (humans) are best at.

We know how to assess a situation, in person, and respond appropriately.

We imagine and create our best work when we crowd-source from each other.

We can invent new ideas and ways to work by watching each other in real time.

Our culture is strongest when we are together on a regular basis.

We can assess new candidates more effectively when we see them in person.

And we'll notice things we would never see on a Zoom call when we are just observing each other in the office.

The storms of change, however, say we should change how we do business and work remotely forever after.

The captain remembers that human beings are not wired that way. If we were, we would have decided to work remotely long ago. But we know it is not as effective. Why?

We build trust with our clients when we do great work and get to know them personally.

We build better careers when we can help our teams navigate their personal growth day by day.

We innovate more when we can whiteboard an idea or play off each other in a conference room. The crowd is always smarter.

We network with current and future clients and our respective teams over meals and drinks.

We get to know each other personally, celebrate the highs, and support each other in the lows.

We're a professional family.
Know any families who decide to live remotely?

CHAPTER 51

READING THE ROOM AND THE ART OF LISTENING

"There is a difference between listening and waiting for your turn to speak."

—*Simon Sinek*

When I was in sales, the process of visiting thirty to forty physicians and other healthcare leaders each week opened my mind to what is possible if we are simply more observant.

I remember being told that Sarasota Memorial Hospital was an account that had not been using our key medical treatments for many years and there was no chance this would change. I had a different view, so I went in and got time with the head of pharmacy. I asked him what he wanted from our company and how I could help him and just listened.

He told me first of his frustrations, then articulated what he wanted, which was more educational material to teach his team, such as our illustrative Netter Atlases, that would help his team. That was it.

So, I provided him with everything he asked for. And he added in our treatments again.

The company was stunned. They were confident they were right. I was told very clearly it could not be done. In this case, I literally did not listen to the advice since I wanted to listen to the customer. That struck me as making the most sense.

Within eighteen months, I was #1 in sales, in part due to this development. I cannot say I had any clever ideas at all, in this case, other than to listen. All the ideas came from customers.

If I combine what we are taught in sales, which is really training in how to engage with other human beings, and add in how this applies in the consulting world, we come up with some remarkably simple next steps that are usually overlooked. Here are my top five:

#1 – Always take notes at every meeting. Whenever we are speaking with a client, current or future, I take notes during the entire conversation for three reasons. First, it is the best way to ensure follow-up is accurate and double-check I heard things correctly. Second, by writing continually, I cannot talk as much. Third, you show respect by writing notes in real time. We must remind young leaders often that they should take notes and not just listen. No one has a good enough memory to recall everything, and clients subtly pick up that you may not care as much if you are not taking notes. When I was a client, if the agency team was not taking notes, I realized their follow-up would be less than optimal. Maybe not always true, but I always thought it.

#2 – Listen at least 50 percent of the time. Any sales trainer will estimate anywhere from 50-80 percent of your time should be spent listening. It does not matter what the number is. The real key is that you are listening to learn, not waiting for your chance to talk. Here are things to watch out for if you love to talk:

If you speak more than 50 percent of the time, slow down.

If you speak in paragraphs rather than headlines, you are probably not as clear in your thinking as you may believe. Slow down.

If you wait to speak all the time, you are probably more concerned with winning your points. You may win, but that is not the point.

Stop, listen, learn, and enjoy the conversation.

#3 – Learn how to read the room. If you walk into an office or see a cube, you can tell a lot about a person by what they put near them.

It could be family photos or books they hope to read or stacks of paper or a perfectly clean desk. How we treat our personal space is a signature of who we are.

Now, when we get into the conference room for a meeting, if you are in listening mode, you are more aware of the dynamics in the room. For example, after being in hundreds, if not thousands, of decision-making meetings, I can usually tell who will make the decision (individual or small team) and the chances of success. The team is transmitting all those signs; we just have to be ready to receive. Just watch how they interact; the clues are all there.

#4 – Embrace tough questions and comments. Some of the most successful accounts in sales started with doctors yelling at me because they were disappointed in the past sales rep (not me). I just listened, learned, and then followed up with their requests. At Dell, we learned that when customers were the most upset with us, it was a form of passion. They cared enough to let us know what mattered to them. If we came through to solve the problem, we had a friend for life. We did many times.

#5 – Always be friends with the whole team. If I wanted to see physicians as a sales rep, I needed to build relationships with the front-office and the nursing teams. Without those, I got nowhere. Every leader has an official or unofficial group that supports them and looks out for them. It is why it is best to be friendly and collegial with everyone you meet.

I remember growing up and my parents pointing out that we should say hello and strike up a conversation with anyone we met, not just our friends. It has led to wonderful conversations with people of all types, allowing me to improve my perspective along the way. It is also just a better way to live.

The conclusion is straightforward.

If you are listening versus waiting to speak, you learn more and are more likely to accurately determine the best future action. And if you show you care via the simplest actions (e.g., taking notes and following up), then you are going to set yourself apart from the many consultants who think every word they say is so important.

It turns out this is not true. Our clients and our peers want to build a productive relationship. They are happy to skip the monologue.

CHAPTER 52

RE-INVENT HOW YOU WORK EVERY DAY

"In today's era of volatility, there is no other way but to re-invent. The only sustainable advantage you can have over others is agility, that's it. Because nothing else is sustainable, everything else you create somebody else will replicate."

—*Jeff Bezos*

The world is constantly evolving. Technology is advancing our abilities. Cultural changes impact how we think and work. Economies ebb and flow from recession to booming markets.

The one guarantee we have in our world is that it will change.

Jeff Bezos, founder of Amazon, knew that if he could create a company that would relentlessly evolve with the marketplace, he could build a special company. Nothing fancy. Nothing so unique that he wins a Nobel Prize. Just a continual focus on how to re-invent the company to align with the needs of the marketplace.

You know the rest of the story.

Today, one of the top annual cloud computing conferences in the world is called "re:Invent," and it is hosted by Amazon Web Services (AWS). The headquarters of AWS, based in Seattle, is called re:Invent. The messaging and mission are clear.

I am not suggesting you rename your office, but there is an uncomplicated way for you to adopt the Bezos way of thinking.

Imagine what you do for clients today. You have standards of work, models of how you do your work, specific ways you build a program, a detailed way of how you deliver creative solutions, and more. You are thoughtful about how you conduct your work.

Great, now take a breath and say this aloud:

> *"Everything I do today is old school. Everything I do will change. I need to figure this out before my competitors do, or I will fall behind."*

That's right. Literally everything you do needs a review.

The good news is the Amazons of the world don't do this overnight. Rather, it is their continual review of how they work that iterates their business. Basically, if you always think like this, you'll keep your edge. If you hold on to the past, well, you will probably not love the outcome someday.

Thinking of what to address first often leads to procrastination, since we are not sure how to get started.

Here is the easiest way I know how, with two examples.

First, look at what you do today and become your own skeptic. An example relates to why we have the name "next practices." If we want to study the past and ensure we are mediocre, the best way to do so is to analyze case studies. Studying the past keeps you there. When reviewing case studies, we realize we are cataloging events that took place in the past to show we know a marketplace or a certain skill. By studying case studies, we are thinking backward and are more apt to repeat the past. A wonderful way to become mediocre. However, if we distill the key insights from a range of case studies, we start to discern patterns that give us an edge in the market, and we realize what the "next practice" may become.

Next step? Abolish case studies. Embrace next practices.

Go through everything you do and be your own skeptic. If you can embrace the fact that what you do today can and should improve, you will get there. If you think this chapter is silly and you are already successful, so there is really no need, well, good luck.

Second, study technology to understand what it is capable of doing.

Many people's instinct is to discount technology as you tell yourself that technology can't do what you can do.

The only problem with that statement is it is not completely accurate.

What about technology that allows someone with no software experience to build a website? What about a software platform to build videos, reports, and decks that can help one person do the work of thirty people? What about software that accelerates how you build a story?

Technology will always need our touch. The question is, are we capable of admitting that some of what we do is actually better when we partner with technology rather than avoid it?

If you dig in and explore what technology can provide, you'll be excited about what you can achieve.

In each case, you will be re-inventing how you work.

Those who re-invent will build a sustainable advantage.

TALENT

CHAPTER 53

THE ART AND SCIENCE OF PRESENTING

"Presentation skills are key. People who work for you represent your brand. You want them to present themselves—and represent you—in a certain way."

—*Marc Benioff*

A great presentation is simple. It's a bit mysterious or even magical. It leaves the audience inspired and eager to move forward.

It's a combination of art and science.

Our goal is to follow that same standard in how we teach how to improve. We won't overcomplicate the art and science of presenting. Rather, we will outline what works and why.

This advice works for your next meeting or the next presentation you are part of. It really relates to any situation where your goal is to articulate what matters and align with your audience, so we can all move forward to support a new idea, campaign, or just lead a productive discussion.

In that spirit, here we go.

The best presenters make it look easy, just like a musician makes it look easy to play the guitar. It's actually not easy at all. These individuals have done it hundreds or thousands of times. They have learned what works and what does not. They have failed and succeeded.

It starts with our own confidence. And it continues with practice.

LEARNING TO BE OURSELVES

Every one of us will raise our hand if asked, "Have you ever been nervous before a presentation?"

It's normal to be anxious if you are going to present. Maybe have the butterflies. And it's actually a great sign. It shows you care. It's energy you can harness, just like musicians or athletes prepare for a concert or a game.

Now, imagine you are going to join an important client meeting tomorrow. You don't have to present, but you do need to introduce yourself and participate.

Here are a few simple ways to address any pre-meeting or pre-presentation jitters:

Study the firm and team you will meet beforehand. You want to come in with thoughts on the company based on your research. Spend time looking at participants' LinkedIn profiles, so you can think about what you might talk about (volunteering, school, work, other).

Strike up a conversation pre-meeting if you can. Share a relevant thought and break the ice early whenever possible.

In the meeting, make your own introduction relevant to the audience. You are invited for a reason. What is it? Figure it out and be proud of sharing. You deserve to be in the room.

Keep it to two or three relevant aspects of your experience. Don't give us your full bio.

And if you are presenting, make sure you have your first thirty to sixty seconds of content nailed down. In doing this, your mind calms down, and you realize you'll be fine. Don't go beyond this, or you become scripted. Just remember enough, so you can dissipate any nervous energy, then get right into being as conversational as you can be.

We all get anxious when we first start presenting. Embrace it and harness this energy.

And remember that the audience is eager to hear from you. They want you to succeed.

BEFORE THE PRESENTATION BEGINS

Preparing Our Presentation

As you prepare the slide deck, imagine you are telling a story versus compiling slides. Here is a simple test to guide you:

Write a headline for each slide that is so clear you don't have to look at the rest of the slide. Now, just read the headlines for each slide for the entire deck and see if the story is compelling. If it isn't, keep editing until it is.

Imagine that our client will not digest all the slides. How could they with so many shown? But they can take in the key point of each slide via your headline.

Each slide provides an insight. Insights can tell a story.

Does it take more time? Yes, in the beginning, but it is what your audience is looking for. No one is thinking, "I hope the headlines are unclear, the slide is dense, and they read it to me." Rather, they just want to hear what is important and keep moving.

When Introducing Yourself in Meetings

Always minimize the time we spend introducing ourselves and our firm. The client can't wait to hear what we have in store for them. Remember to share two to three things about yourself, not five or six. Don't meander. Be clear and brief.

Think of a ticking clock. Imagine you have only a few minutes to grab their attention. Why would we take a long time to introduce ourselves and the firm? The only reason we would is if we want to lose focus, not gain it. Keep it simple.

When we introduce ourselves, share what is relevant to the client. Don't repeat what the person next to you said. Be original.

Too many times, we hear, "Hi, I'm XYZ. I have been at the firm for three years. I graduated from X college. I worked at Y place and so on." Why not say, "Hi, I'm XYZ," and then provide two reasons why your experience matches up with the client's needs?

How to Create Memorable Slides

One idea per slide. Not three. Not two. One.

Never pack in lots of content so you feel better. No one wants to read this much.

A simple idea doesn't need more time in the deck. Don't push content onto a slide. Let the slide breathe and express one idea.

Case Studies versus Key Learnings

Every case study from every firm sounds the same! We are amazing. Our results were awesome. We received unbelievable coverage. We are the best!

Just like every other firm on the planet!

Everyone knows we congratulate ourselves during case studies.

Our answer? Don't call them case studies, and don't fall into this trap.

Share key learnings from the examples. Highlight one to two key insights. That's it. Move to the next one. And only show examples that are relevant.

Volume does not win the day. Saying we are awesome doesn't either.

But when a client can see we are thinking, iterating, and learning, now that's a team you want on your side as a client. Show how our experience shapes us!

The Differentiation Test

Ask yourself a simple question: If twenty other agencies were given our slides, could they put their name on our deck and would it basically work? If so, we aren't ready. Our decks should be unique to us every time. Yep, that means how we present our experience, our offering, our ideas, our learnings. The entire deck.

Can we say why it is unique? If we do, we separate from the pack and clients notice.

Reading the Room and How We Present Ourselves

When you walk into the room, how do you show up?

Do you stand up and shake everyone's hand? If not, why? Showing respect is important each and every time.

Where do you sit? Do you cluster with your team, or do you spread out and sit next to one of your clients? This shows confidence. If you all sit together, this is kind of odd. Spread out.

Who will make the decision in the room? What's the hierarchy of the client team? What else do you notice, and why does it matter?

Learning how to read a room starts with being self-aware, taking note of who is there, how they act, what they say, and more.

THE MEETING BEGINS

A member of the client starts speaking. And you start taking notes. You are an active notetaker for two reasons. One is that you can retain what is said for later, and it is a form of brainstorming. The second is you are showing recognition and respect. When you don't take notes, your subconscious message to the speaker is, "I am not interested enough to take notes on what you are saying." Always take notes.

When clients see that you aren't taking notes, they assume you are distracted or simply don't care. Or you are too excited about your own thinking that you aren't listening to their ideas.

When we must write down our notes, it slows us down. It helps us brainstorm in the moment. Often, the best ideas are an offshoot of a conversation. And those same notes may help us later in the meeting if we decide to lead a whiteboard session, for example.

The Flow of the Presentation

Do you know anyone who likes to hear a completely controlled presentation? No? Didn't think so. We like to be in a conversation. And there is a significant difference in presentation styles.

The classic presentation style is to tell each person, "You do slides one through four, then you do slides five through eight, then you handle nine through twelve," and so on. What this leads to is a scripted performance. Clients can see it is scripted, and they don't love it.

The best presentation style is like a real conversation. You still have your sections, but you talk with each other during the presentation. You may add to someone else's thoughts, ask questions of the audience, and might even whiteboard some ideas on the spot.

One style infers we are very careful and cautious. The other style infers we are creative and strategic.

So, how do we know if we are being too scripted? It is ok to plan. Planning helps us get fluent with the material. It helps us know which person is the expert in each area. And it helps us with our timing. So, continue planning.

But don't make it obvious you did. Be conversational. Make it ok for one person to comment while another is speaking. React to client questions on the spot. Pivot in the presentation whenever you need to. Go with the flow.

No one has ever received an award (or business) for finishing their deck. It is our ability to tell a powerful story that leads to success. If you never finish a complete slide deck the rest of your life, kudos to you. Your clients will love you!

One Idea, One Slide, One Minute

If you need to take more than one minute to explain a slide, it is too long. Focus on one idea per slide for one minute or less. And to illustrate that point, think of how our brains process information. When you show a slide, our brains immediately read what's on it. We're done, and you're still discussing the concept or idea.

Now, if you are focused on one idea, and the slide is focused on one idea, you make it easy to comprehend. If you are going on and on in a long thread about the topic, and the audience read the slide two minutes ago, they are more than likely daydreaming about something else. You lost them.

Stay focused.

Great presenters realize it takes time for new ideas to settle in our brains. Make it easy to take them in. Repeat those ideas in different ways to reinforce the core thoughts throughout your presentation. You'll be glad you did.

Anticipate the Questions You Will Be Asked

It's pretty easy to figure out most of the questions we'll be asked. "Who will lead the team?" "Who is on the team today?" "How much will this cost?" "When will this be completed?" Things like that.

Great presenting teams have already addressed these questions before they say their first word. Good teams are ready to answer. Mediocre teams say they will follow up with more detail or some answer that shows they were not ready.

If you hesitate, the audience assumes you don't know, even if your future answer is good. When you know, you know.

Practice before you walk in the room. The questions are rarely a surprise.

Remember Why the Audience Is There

The audience, often our client, is there because they hope to improve their brand or company. Are we addressing this throughout the presentation? It's a yes or no. If not a clear yes, rethink the approach.

If you were the client, why would you be thrilled to have just heard this presentation? Why was it worth your time? Be specific.

If you can't answer this question, rethink your approach.

Remember What the Audience Wants to Do

The audience wants to hear about its situation and how we will address it. So, here is a quick rule to follow: Look at your presentation and determine how much of the deck is directly solving the client's problem and how much is "filler." Do you have the right percentage? The answer is as close to 100 percent of the former as possible.

Here is another way to think about it: The perfect client presentation is nearly 100 percent about the client. Look at your presentation and ask how much time is spent on you. Is that the best use of your time? How do you get closer to 80/20, for example?

Focus on Your Listening Skills

It takes practice to listen well. Here's why: It is active listening that works the best. We are thinking of what questions we can ask to stimulate conversation. We ask questions to probe and learn more about what a client desires. We ask questions to confirm if we are going in the right direction.

Great questions lead a discussion. Mediocre questions are asked so we can show we are asking questions, but don't advance the agenda.

It is often said that the best CEOs are the best at asking questions. They are constantly learning from us, even if they may already feel like they have the answer. They always want to understand our perspective. Their questions make us think about what else we could be doing.

They are moving us forward by a question, not a command.

That is powerful listening. So, if you are not asking questions, consider it half-listening. Move to full listening. And ask yourself if your questions move us forward or not?

Build on the Ideas of Others

Doesn't it feel good when someone says, "I would like to add to what Brittany said?" It sure does, since it shows an awareness of what was said before, and it shows respect for the idea.

When we are building momentum for our ideas or campaigns, we are also building buy-in with the audience, and that accelerates if we all feel like a team.

To feel like a team, act like one. Ensure the contributions of team members are real. Share the wealth.

But Don't Overbuild

You have been in meetings when the third person and then the fourth all chime in to share their thoughts that they are in solidarity with the first person who chimed in.

What's the purpose?

The answer is there isn't one. When someone else has answered a question well, be satisfied. Move on. Only add in if you truly add insight that makes the response more powerful.

Otherwise, as hard as it may be, don't speak.

Know When You Are Talking Too Much

If you speak in paragraphs, that's often too much. Here is an easy way to assess yourself:

- Are you known for asking questions to stimulate conversation? Or are you known for simply waiting to say something when others are speaking?
- This impacts how our brains work. Our real goal in each meeting is to advance our agenda.

- We don't get extra points for talking a lot. We are rewarded by the outcome we achieve, both in the meeting and outside of it.
- Stay focused on achieving the outcome. And think twice if you hear yourself talking too much, even if everyone is smiling.
- Time yourself. Many leaders speak too much since no one ever tells them to stop.

Self-awareness can do wonders for future conversations.

Always Stand

Too often, we hear people say, "Oh, are you going to sit? Yeah, me too." Wrong. For several reasons.

First, it is easier for our lungs to work when we are standing up, which helps us breathe and speak more clearly, more powerfully, and often with less anxiety.

Second, it is a position that gives you a command of the room. And it shows respect.

Even when others say they will sit, you can still get up and speak.

Plus, when we walk around, people are more aware. When we point to a slide, we pay attention. We keep the audience on their toes if we are on our toes as well.

Answer First, Not Last

The scientific method starts with an introduction and carefully follows a path to a conclusion. This might work for *The New England Journal of Medicine*, but it is ineffective as a presentation technique. A model built by Bain Consulting, called Answer First, literally summarizes the plan in the first slide. This way, the audience knows what is coming. Your future slides build on the first. Even when you are preparing a surprise, you can still do a version of Answer First to set the scene.

Always take control by setting the scene.

And, if for some reason you don't have an Answer-First slide at the beginning of your next deck, create one for yourself anyway. This process instills in you what your strategy is, what the key messages are, and why this approach matters.

Don't forget to do this every time. Clients count on us every time.

Effective Ways to Sell

An audience doesn't do as well if they are sitting for twenty to thirty minutes, waiting for the big reveal. That heightens the risk an idea will be accepted. An audience prefers a rhythm where they are continually agreeing with you, often subconsciously, as you make each point. Imagine five to six moments in a deck where the audience thinks, "Yes, that makes sense. I hadn't thought of that or didn't realize they could do that." And if that is the momentum you are building, you are preparing the path to acceptance.

Here are some examples of those moments: You have insights from analytics. You show a unique media model. You show how you will build a story. You have a few bigger ideas. It's a culmination of this type of thinking that wows a client. Although it can happen, it is rarely just one big idea.

Feature, Advantage, and Benefit (FAB)

Selling techniques are as old as the hills. Yet, we rarely study them and often don't realize what we are missing. Here is a powerful and simple model:

FAB it.

When you introduce a feature, always include an advantage and its benefit to the client. For example, too often, clients hear, "We have one of the best media relations teams in the business." They are thinking, "So what." But, if you say, "We believe our media relations team is one of the best teams for your firm, since three team members worked in category X and know the top twenty reporters, which gives us an ability to understand which stories are of most interest to their outlets and your firm."

One pats us on the back. The other explains to a client why our team is a good fit.

Most of what we say falls into the feature category. Always stretch and ask what the advantage of what we do is and why it will provide a direct benefit to our client.

In sales, when you do this, you close. When you forget to do it, you have great conversations with people who often really like you, but nothing happens.

Kind of like when a client says, "We really like your firm, the people are great, but we went with firm X."

How to Close

We are told that closing means you "ask for the business." You can, but that's not really the most effective close.

Closing is really a concept. It means the "buyer" is convinced they should work with you. What this means is that if you provide five to six unique moments throughout a thirty-to-forty-five-minute presentation, you are showing up well as a team. You are prepared for all the questions. What you are really doing is closing one step at a time, so by the end, you don't really close. The client is already convinced.

If you make a forty-five-minute presentation and then feel a need to ask for the business, it's probably because you did a poor job closing in the forty-five minutes prior.

It's not a question or statement to make at the end. It's the process.

HOW TO FOLLOW UP

You just finished a great meeting. Everyone seems happy. Conversation is flowing.

Too often, we think this means we are done, and one of us will send a follow-up email in the next day or two. This is the standard.

But follow-up starts right away. Imagine presenting, and then as you are wrapping up, you do the following:

You provide a favorite book (one we wrote or just a favorite) that is relevant to the discussion.

You provide a handout of the presentation.

Then think through how you might follow up in a unique way. Could you do something that is unique to the customer? For example, is their additional research to show the client? Or is there just something funny you could send? Or you follow up with an email that has some additional links with key information for further reading?

The key point is you take time to think through if and how you can make an impact in your follow-up.

MORE ON HOW TO PRACTICE AND PREPARE

Working the Whiteboard

It can be compelling to stand up during a presentation, react to the discussion, and whiteboard an idea. Of course, to make this impactful, it must be natural, which means you need to practice whiteboarding concepts on your own, so it's effortless when you do it. Just like practicing presentations.

Slideshow Karaoke

This is a great exercise to practice speaking agility. When you are practicing, use a slide show that has ten to fifteen random slides. It is your job to stand up (without seeing the slides) and create a story on the spot related to what you see. This forces us to think on our feet, develop transitions to new ideas, and build a compelling story we tell with confidence.

You will also laugh quite a bit as you practice. It's fun. It also helps you be more conversational when you present.

The Power of a Written Narrative

Sometimes we can't articulate a concept in full during a presentation. There may not be enough time, or the concept is one that takes time to understand. Don't "hope" it works. Write out a narrative you can hand to the client as you speak during the presentation. Keep it to one page and clearly articulate the concept. This illustrates that you view the concept/idea as important, and it's something the client can read later to further understand.

When to Use Handouts

Handouts emphasize what you believe is important. Use them when you want to make a point. Don't give them out if they don't achieve this goal.

When to Have a Hybrid Call (and When Not To)

Our job is to inform and influence our audience so that we can move forward with the ideas/campaign we created. If you believe people who are remote will add value to the presentation, utilize them, but remember that even if they are more senior than you, they cannot read the room like you can.

So, talk about this pre-meeting. Agree on who will give an audible if the conversation needs to shift or we're going too slow in our slides. A person in the room looking eye to eye with the client team needs to have this authority, independent of title.

What Is the Right Team?

Start by knowing who from the client will be in the room and how you match up best with this in-person team. Then, think through who will work on the team. And from there, you can figure out the right mix.

Always strive not to overwhelm or underwhelm a client based on the size or makeup of your team. Just "whelm them."

Sometimes too many senior people might be off-putting. Sometimes too junior a team may not show the experience we need to display.

Imagine what the client wants and build that team. Don't build the team based on people's desire to be in the room. Do it based on your view of the client's needs.

LEADERSHIP INSIGHT

The Courage to Build

Startups cost money before they become profitable. So do new practices. So do new firms. So does anything of future value.

The best entrepreneurs know how to take risk and reduce it simultaneously.

In a service business, we focus on our pipeline of opportunities, so we can judge how quickly we can hire, since we have to hire ahead of the curve. In a software start-up, we often take money from friends and family to see if our idea can get off the ground and start to earn its keep.

A new practice is only a cool idea until we hire people, build an offering, and make available what we do.

It takes courage.

Most leaders kill innovation in its tracks due to their allergy to investment.

They only think of profit and loss as it impacts them today, yet anything of value requires at least a three-to-five-year mindset.

So, what does it mean to have the courage to build?

It means you continue to invest in your new firm, even if you lost money the first or second year, as long as you can see other indicators of success, e.g., revenue growth, client acceptance, etc.

It means you lead with patience and a belief that your leaders will achieve their business.

If you challenge every detail of your investment out of the gate, you won't build much of anything.

Agree on the vision. Get the right leaders in place. Have the courage to invest, build, and benefit from your ability to be patient, disciplined, and focused on what you will create.

Imagine success in three years, not three months.

CHAPTER 54

THE ART OF THE INTRODUCTION

"You never get a second chance to make a first impression."

— Will Rogers

The meeting starts, everyone is in a great mood, and we start the ceremony of introductions. No one has prepared for this part of the meeting, so you hear the usual.

"Hi, my name is XYZ. I have been at the firm for eleven months. And I focus on financial services."

Then the next person.

"Hi, my name is ABC. And I have been at the firm for two years. I focus on media relations."

It goes something like this. No thought given to what the audience needs to hear. And the group starts following a pattern.

When I was a client, I would half-listen and start to think, "I'm not sure this firm sees us as special. Maybe they aren't as good as I thought."

So, I'm starting the meeting thinking this may be the wrong choice. The firm is thrilled they all introduced themselves.

Remember there is an art to introducing oneself. Here's what we recommend doing:

Take the time to look at the LinkedIn profile of each attendee.

Review the client's business and line up your specific experience with their company's products and services.

It sounds something like this:

"Hi, I'm Sally Smith. I graduated from the University of Texas at Austin with a business degree, which I believe you did as well, Ralph. I have been fortunate to work on fraud protection for several years working for the US government, and I have represented two of the top trade associations in the authentication space. In my spare time, I am involved with an effort to protect the identities of foster children, utilizing the technology of our industry."

Ralph responds, "Cool, when were you at UT? I graduated in '96 from McCombs."

Another client responds, "Where in the government did you work? And can we talk after this about what you are doing for foster children?"

You answer, "Sure, I graduated in 2000. Loved McCombs. I worked for NSA for four years. And yes, I would love to talk about how we protect foster kids. We could use some help."

The result is a conversation that started from an introduction. A relationship is forming. And your client or future client is starting to think that maybe this team is more special than most.

If you do your homework, it will show and your client will appreciate your effort. Who knows what topics of conversation you may spark through your preparation!

CHAPTER 55

THE IMPORTANCE OF COACHING

"A coach is someone who can give correction without causing resentment."

—John Wooden

My father, also named Bob, was an exceptional athlete (minor league shortstop for the NY Yankees) and then served as the baseball coach for our town for decades, in addition to being a physical education teacher.

When my brother and I were kids, we would often get to ride the bus to games with the players and then watch our team, Millburn High School, play our rivals. We had a bird's-eye view of how our dad coached his team.

Long after he retired, our dad would hear from players who called or visited him at home to share what they were doing in life and thank him for the impact he made in their lives.

It was these moments that made me realize how coaching a sport is more than winning a game. What my dad was really doing was teaching life skills to teenagers through the prism of a game.

Looking back, here is what we learned from Coach Pearson:

#1 – Great coaching leads to great practice. If you needed to learn how to hit the ball up the middle of the infield, my dad might focus on the position of your elbow as you swung the bat. He would stay focused on getting this right, so that you could practice it for days and weeks after his instruction.

Learning: *If you provide advice that can improve how a person can practice when you are not around, you have succeeded. If you dump out all your thinking and they don't know what to do once you leave, you failed. Focus on one improvement at a time.*

#2 – Show how to do something. If you could not understand his message, he would show you. My dad would pick up the bat, show the right stance, and hit the ball up the middle.

Learning: *Be a practitioner, not just a pontificator.*

#3 – A quick affirmation you are on the right track matters. When a player made the right swing motion, they needed to hear they succeeded, which helped them lock in on the right behavior.

Learning: *We all need affirmation that we are making progress.*

#4 – New skills often take months to perfect. When we can't improve right away, talk about why it is difficult. For example, when I first learned to throw a curve ball as a pitcher, I had to understand how to grip the ball and snap my wrist to get the best break in the pitch. My dad would find what I was doing well, keep showing me how to do the pitch, and teach me how to practice. Eventually, I got there.

Learning: *Be clear when new skills will take time versus instant success.*

#5 – Don't allow emotion to highjack your mind. When you make an error in the infield, do you think about it continually and mess up your ability to concentrate when you are next at bat? Or can you place these thoughts out of your mind? My dad taught us how to learn from the moment, but also how to let it go.

Learning: *Teach yourself to compartmentalize your thoughts by reminding yourself that negative thoughts have never helped anyone succeed. Get them out of your brain quickly.*

#6 – Think about how you support your teammates. How you present yourself can inspire or deflate your team. We learned the "banter" of baseball, where you continually call out words of encouragement to your teammates during the game.

Learning: No one ever complained they received too much backing from their team, not just the coach, the team.

#7 – Do your homework, so your anticipation provides an edge. What is the pitcher likely to throw me next if the count is 2-0 versus 3-2 versus 0-2? If you really watch your competitors and imagine how they think, you can often anticipate what they will do next.

Learning: *How often do we imagine what our competitors will do in a new business presentation and then outthink them?*

#8 – A loss teaches you what to do better next time. That simple. Figure out what you learned and then improve. In baseball, we would figure out why we didn't turn a routine grounder into a double play and then practice how to do it right fifty times until we nailed the process.

Learning: *Ask yourself how you practice to get better in areas you are not as strong. If you know how you could have improved, did you fix the process, improve the slides, or make a change? Or did you just admit it and not really do anything new?*

#9 – Every detail really does matter. Competitors in sports take advantage of each mistake we make. Their goal that day is to beat us, clear and simple.

Learning: *When we can't see competitors, we assume everything is fine, but they are trying to take our business every single day. What are they thinking about today?*

#10 – The team always comes first, never the individual. You take every action to make your team better. You are just a part of that team. How you support each other makes the difference.

Learning: *There isn't really such a thing as an individual contributor. We are all teammates, just playing different and important roles that play off each other. Know how you contribute and why it's valuable, and you can make an impact.*

My dad was known for being highly competitive, and yet his players loved him and visited him right up until he passed away at the age of ninety-two.

He would teach us how to slide to break up a double play, but then be the first person to congratulate the other team when we finished playing.

He practiced relentlessly to be the best and would give his heart and soul to anyone who would do the same. But he had no time for slackers.

He knew that no matter how much talent we may start with, the kid or coach in the next neighborhood also has similar skills. It's often the team who comes in more prepared, more aware of their competitors, and works seamlessly to support each other who ends up with the victory. Chemistry matters.

We were taught the lessons of life and business on a ball field every day. We just didn't realize it at the time.

That meant we also helped each other off the field. Not everyone's life was going perfectly (it rarely is), and he was there for the kid who may have been down in the dumps because his parents never came to see them pitch, their parents were breaking up, or they were having trouble in school, and so were we.

What we learned was helpful on the base paths of the diamond, as it has been in the hallways of the biggest companies. Each lesson was learned one pitch and one practice at a time.

And that is why grown men visited with Coach Pearson decades after he coached them to check in, see how he was doing, and let him know that what they learned helped them become someone their family is proud of today.

Thanks Dad.

CHAPTER 56

THE SHIFT FROM COMPETENCE TO CONFIDENCE

"Competence is a great creator of confidence."

—*Mary Jo Putney*

A twenty-two-year-old fresh out of university walks into a conference room for their first client meeting.

An account supervisor is about to make her first presentation to the whole client team and then has to lead an hour-long session.

A senior vice president is about to walk on stage to address three hundred industry peers and present for twenty minutes.

A newly appointed leader is getting ready to hold their first all hands to talk about the practice they now lead.

Each scenario represents a first. One that probably played in our heads for days or weeks prior to that day as we thought about what we would do and how we would be perceived.

Well, what have we learned from thousands of client presentations and hundreds of industry talks and all hands?

We've learned that there are no short cuts. You should not wing it. You can excel in all these situations if you focus on building your level of competence throughout your career. It is a commitment that really never ends, until your career itself ends.

Here are a few ways you can build competence that translates into confidence:

Act like a client—Your client is thinking about their business every day. You should, too. Read their trade publications. Study their analyst reports. Imagine you will be asked to brief the firm on your client. Could you explain their business in a fluent manner if the client's CEO called you right now?

Learn how to sell—We are in the business of selling a story, a concept, an idea, a campaign. This is selling, whether we want to admit it or not. Read the top books on selling. Focus on the most basic sales skills, such as knowing how to "FAB it," which means when you share an idea, you provide the "feature," the "advantage," and the "benefit" all in one statement. Set out to become an expert in selling. What are three learnings you will put into practice this year? How about next year?

Read to learn—Continually select topics that will increase your knowledge and push yourself, just like you did in school. Read about search engine optimization or China or artificial intelligence or the history of storytelling. Imagine that you are in school forever and just keep learning. A broad base of knowledge improves your ability to generate ideas, think on your feet, and lead conversations in a productive direction.

Here's the punchline on why these areas matter so much:

The answer is a mix of competence and confidence that sets you apart over time.

Clients love consultants who go deep and understand their business. You become more of a peer than a vendor.

Clients want to understand why any action is worth doing. Great sales skills make this easy to do, and meetings seem almost effortless.

Your peers in the industry are always interested in learning from a person who can make them think. And clients seek out those who will give them new ideas on a regular basis.

The result of this approach is you become more intellectually agile in any situation. You know the business. You know what should be done. You know what's around the corner. You can't wait for the next meeting.

It is this level of competence that leads to the confidence that defines great leaders.

Malcolm Gladwell said that it takes ten thousand hours to become an expert in an area. If we think of a work year as two thousand hours, we all realize it takes time to become an expert in anything.

Great consultants are patient, persistent, and keep learning.

It is this journey that builds our competence and allows our confidence to shine through.

CHAPTER 57

THE VALUE AND IMPORTANCE OF OUR REVIEWS

"Your talent determines what you can do.
Your motivation determines how much you are willing to do.
Your attitude determines how well you do it."

—*Lou Holtz*

We have been thinking through the thousands of reviews we have collectively been part of, both as the recipient and the leader, in our careers. More importantly, we continually ask people from entry level to firm veterans what really matters during a review throughout our industry.

It is easy to make a review too complex. Or, perhaps, not spend enough time thinking through what really matters. The good news is this is easy to avoid.

If we get down to basics, it's pretty clear what the person getting reviewed is wondering about in the weeks before, during, and after the review. If we address these areas in a meaningful way, we will provide the best counsel and make the most impact on team members who are important to our teams and firm.

Here are the key areas to think about as you prepare for your next review, whether you are being reviewed or are the reviewer:

OURSELVES – How Am I Actually Doing?

- What am I doing well?
- What can I improve on, and more importantly, what steps should I take?
- What training should I consider improving?

RELATIONSHIPS – How Can I Figure Out How to Do Well in Our Firm?

- How can I improve the relationship with you, my manager? Do you accept two-way feedback?
- Do I feel comfortable asking for your time to teach me? What does that look like going forward?
- How am I doing building relationships throughout the firm? How can I improve?

MY CAREER – What Is the Next Step, and Is It Clear and Achievable?

- What is my merit and bonus increase? How does that reflect how you view my work?
- What is my next step to be promoted? Any idea on the potential timing if my performance is strong?

Overall, what is continually reinforced is that the process itself is straightforward. If we speak to the topics important to the person we are reviewing, our teammate is far more likely to internalize the feedback, see it as helpful, and put it into action in the months/years ahead. If your team member feels like we are talking in a highly sophisticated manner, using charts and numbers, and getting too clinical, we actually lose our ability to make the most impact.

Keep it simple and imagine yourself in their seat as you lead the discussion. And remember, the best reviews are a conversation that leads to specific insights and next steps.

LEADERSHIP INSIGHT

The Value of Shared Services

You are an entrepreneur building a business. Something you do is really valuable to your clients. Why would you think you are also equally as good at understanding finance, human resources, legal, real estate, and other key areas of operations?

- *Can you build integrated spreadsheets that analyze cash flow over the next five years?*
- *How strong are you at analyzing your real estate footprint?*
- *Are you trained in how to negotiate legal contracts or put them together?*
- *How often are you the lead person with procurement, and should you be?*
- *Are you an expert in the most recent standards for cybersecurity to protect your firm?*

You know the answer.

Your shared services team should be as high quality a team as your best client service team.

Invest in all aspects of your business. You'll be glad you did.

CHAPTER 58

WHAT EXACTLY ARE WE "REVIEWING" DURING REVIEWS?

"Your past is not your potential. In any hour, you can choose to liberate the future."

—*Marilyn Ferguson*

The annual review process is antiquated. Let's retire it.

Thank you. You sort of worked, but your time is over. Bye-bye.

The reviews we need demand we rethink why we do it at all.

We cannot go back in time and change what occurred last year or last month or yesterday.

We can shape the future, inspire our leaders to improve their skills, offer new experiences, and challenge each team member to improve continually.

This is what a powerful review accomplishes.

Before we go further, I would like to reflect on a lesson I learned from Michael Dell about what we choose to celebrate.

When I was working at Dell, teams repeatedly asked me if we could celebrate that they reached a certain milestone. Have cakes in the cafeteria, maybe bring in a band, and talk about their achievement. The usual stuff.

Reluctantly, I brought one of these ideas to Michael, who listened, then said, "Why would you celebrate the past?"

Like many points Michael made, that question opened my eyes. What we need to celebrate is the future we can create together.

And that is the real purpose of a review.

With this in mind, a template emerges that you can customize for your firm. Here is the one we use ourselves. It has seven parts, and it leads to active follow-up throughout the year to check on progress.

#1 – Last year's learnings – We briefly reflect on what worked and what did not with equal vigor. We identify the strengths we want to continue to enhance and the weaknesses that require more practice. We should outline at least two of each, not five or ten. Keep it simple.

Note: *If you only focus on the positives, you have conducted a poor review. Candor leads to improvement. We can all ALWAYS improve.*

#2 – New skills – What new skill will you work on this year? What current skill can you improve, and what will you do to improve?

Note: *Be clear and write out your next steps pre-review.*

#3 – New experience – Will you move to a different team? New office? New industry? What will you do to expand your experience base?

Note: *It may not happen the next year, but share your personal vision.*

#4 – Networking – How often will you meet people external to your firm for a meal or a drink? What outside organizations will you participate in?

Note: *Start with at least one meeting or special call per month and get to where you do it weekly. The leaders who build firms all do this well.*

#5 – Giving back – What can you do this year to make our world a better place? It can be remarkably simple but should be something.

Note: *"I don't have enough time" is an excuse. Figure out what you can do every year.*

#6 – Reading – What do you read today, and how do you learn? How will you improve how you learn?

Note: *Push yourself to read in new areas. Create your own information edge.*

#7 – Next position – What is the next position you expect to receive? What do you need to do to achieve this goal? What is a reasonable timeframe? How will you check in with your leader during the year to discuss your progress?

> ***Note:*** *You should know what you need to do and be able to speak honestly with your manager about your progress. Promotions should not just be handed out. Learn how to earn them.*

If we turn a review into an opportunity to briefly reflect and focus on one's future, both the reviewer and reviewee walk away inspired and have a game plan to follow.

If we turn the review into a session of compliments and not much else, it feels good, but we quickly realize it didn't add a lot of value.

We owe it to our teams, as leaders, to unlock their potential, which we accomplish by liberating their future.

OPERATIONS

CHAPTER 59

@SUM(NUMBERS+PEOPLE+CLIENTS/COST)=INSIGHTS

EMBRACE MATH

"To rush into explanations is always a sign of weakness."

—*Agatha Christie,* The Seven Dials Mystery

Whether we are consulting in a firm or within a company, we are often primed to "respond with speed." We are told that "moving fast" matters. "It's ok to make mistakes." Things like that.

That's sort of right, but it's missing a fairly important point.

When you understand the math of your business, you are able to play chess, not checkers, in how you build your team and firm.

A consulting firm is pretty easy to figure out. Our biggest strength (and cost) is our team. Our expenses are generally related to supporting our team (healthcare, real estate, training), investing in finding new clients (new business), or adding new platforms (financial, HR, IT).

The difficult part is figuring out when we should hire ahead of the curve. Or when we need to make a tough call based on performance. Or when we should raise our prices.

All these decisions are easier if we understand the math of our business.

Inside a company, it can be more obscure, since our function rolls up to another function that rolls up to another function. It can feel like the unfolding of the universe sometimes. So, what can we control in either situation?

We can and should know the full cost of our team and be able to place a value on our team's output versus our cost, so that we can show how our output could evolve if we grow. We might call it ROI inside a company, but it's really output and results we're talking about.

In consulting, this explains why we ask about billable hours. Percentages are directional, but not all that helpful. A math-oriented leader asks, "What is the actual revenue per person for the year?" which multiplies hours billed by hourly rate. This is what matters.

In a company, we care about the completion of key tasks. Having lots to do is nice, but points on the board combined with results are what matter. We launched a new website dedicated to the environment and are now getting ten thousand new visitors per month. Results that are tangible. Not, "We completed the website." Who cares?

As a leader, you can tell who knows their numbers, since they explain the context of their decisions or requests in a manner that resonates with how the leadership team looks at the world.

Leaders say things like, "Based on our current staff makeup, I believe we need to hire XYZ," or "I believe we should offer this service as a product for $40,000 rather than bill by the hour, and here is why."

Leaders know that math helps us get to a decision far faster. Intangible beliefs and ideas not tethered to numbers often remain untethered.

Whether you are consulting or inside a company, there is a very simple model.

It's referred to as the pyramid model and shows the span of each leader's responsibility. We always want the most people at entry level. It tapers off with each level for a simple reason: strong leaders can manage growing teams. If you look more like a rectangle, well, you aren't building the best team.

These leaders say, "You don't understand. We must have senior leaders on all of our assignments."

But we do understand, since this is one of the excuses used by leaders who are avoiding people they can manage (maybe they don't like managing) or are fearful of hiring people smarter than they are at any level (believing it diminishes their value).

Math and some good coaching can help these leaders see what they need to do.

We can help these leaders understand who to hire and how to incentivize their teams and break this pattern of self-dependency.

If you ignore math, then you are probably not destined for the C-suite. Your decisions will become increasingly risky to the business if they are not centered on how your decisions improve the business.

Profitable businesses make it possible for the best compensation systems, career development paths, and robust offerings. In a sense, as a leader, you owe it to your team to learn your way around a spreadsheet.

The good news is that no one has ever died from learning math, even if you didn't like it in school. Broken into a sweat? Sure, but nothing more. Plus, you are likely surrounded by a very capable finance team who will be glad to help you learn more.

Embrace math and help yourself become the best leader you can be.

LEADERSHIP INSIGHT

What Successful People Are Really Like

My dad played AAA baseball, as you know from prior chapters, for the New York Yankees and was our baseball coach in high school. He taught us how to critique ourselves every day, so we could learn what we did well and repeat it and do the same for what we were not doing well.

It is this constant improvement mentality that successful people all have in common.

If you ask them if they are the best at something, they deflect. That's not really the point.

If you ask them if they are great leaders, they tell you what they need to improve.

If you ask them if they are satisfied with their careers, they point out what they will do next.

If you ask them what they are learning, they can tell you.

Successful people don't let compliments slow them down and never believe they are as good as they can be tomorrow.

CHAPTER 60

GLOBAL EXPANSION—WHAT MATTERS FOR NEW MARKETS AND WHY

"Only those who will risk going too far can possibly find out how far one can go."

— *T.S. Eliot*

First impressions are often long lasting. When we expand into a new geography and open an office, do we embrace the community we are joining or just hang a shingle? In general, whether it is a new geography or a new market or a new anything, once you decide to go forward, go all in.

Our team has been involved in leading global communications for Fortune 500 companies. We have developed a set of key learnings important for us as we look to expand into new markets, whether it is a geographic move, a shift in where R&D occurs, a decision to change where a regional office is located, or other moves that show we value a new area of the world. Here is a brief summary:

FIVE KEY LEARNINGS

Emphasize the value of the new location. In your news release and overall outreach, share why the new location is important to the future of your company. Whether it is the talent available or the city/country's history of innovation or something else, find something to celebrate unique to this location. Think of what will resonate to the people who live there. If you don't, it comes across as another dot on the map to the locals.

Explain to your core market why expansion is valuable. Your existing following of journalists, thought leaders, and investors in your home country are also wondering why you are making this move at this specific time. The "value" may answer this question, but make sure it's clear enough as you write the narrative.

Who you make available to the media matters. If the CEO is available for key interviews, you are sending a clear message of commitment. If you don't, you are sending a message that this is sort of important. A great way to think of it is like a dialogue. Will your CEO engage in interviews and conferences that show a commitment to this new area? This shows how important or unimportant a location may be.

Who you brief matters more than the coverage. Coverage is certainly a measure of acceptance, but so is showing respect to new leaders in the market you are entering. You might speak with journalists who won't cover the story this time, let local officials know this is an important move for your company, or brief other key thought leaders in the city/country. It can feel like "too much extra time," but it's also why those who make an effort to get to know their new "neighbors" make a real impact. Think and act long term. This is often forgotten.

Don't be a stranger. Now that you have announced, what will you do over the next twelve to eighteen months to show momentum? Will you announce new hires or key leaders joining? Will certain aspects of your development occur here? Think of what you can talk about. Think about what you can sponsor if there are key events. Think about a conference you could speak at in the country. Think of how to show that this city/country is now part of your regular world.

These are the five key learnings that we have found make a real difference. It's all part of building relationships that will benefit your company and the city/country you are now part of.

CHAPTER 61

FIND NEW WAYS TO SCREW UP

"Creativity is seeing what others see and thinking what no one else ever thought."

—*Albert Einstein*

Albert Einstein never met a box he couldn't think outside of. It's a mindset that propels us to not be tied to conventional thinking.

We often associate this approach with creativity and talk about "out of the box" ideas. It is our continual search for the "big idea."

But creativity is not only the domain of the artist. It is equally useful for teams whose job it is to protect us, whether it is from bad actors or bad decisions.

For example, when we think about how to deal with bad actors who may target a company, it is most helpful if we imagine we are the bad actors and plan the attack. This frees our mind and enables us to get creative, think of how to circumvent a company's world, and imagine how we would wreak havoc. And from there, we effectively plan.

It's a mindset that can lead to an ability to routinely plan, spot, and fix problems in an agile manner.

One of the more important uses of this mindset involves a team that is working on client solutions every day across all industries. And it's one you might not think of right away, either because you are outsourcing this work and have no idea how apps are being developed for you or you haven't had this type of discussion with your in-house team.

It is the world of DevOps.

Our DevOps team, which is responsible for accelerating our client's ability to deliver software applications to the world, lives with a mindset that they refer to as "finding new ways to screw up."

They imagine what can go wrong.

Then they imagine what will go wrong based on that mistake.

They take a sip of coffee and brainstorm on what errors could occur during a build.

Later on, over a beer, they keep thinking about the most absurd scenarios of how a project can get screwed up.

Believe me. It happens.

Teams of developers have created "holding content" that accidently goes live.

Sometimes a back door is created to use during development, but the door isn't closed, which can make it easier to hack a site later on.

In regulated industries, a team might skip an important step that impacts the privacy of key information.

The list goes on.

And that list includes security, confidentiality of information, dealing with broken code, incompatibility of different forms of software, changing requirements, syntax or logic errors in code, and much more.

Our job is to imagine it all going south and ensuring this never happens.

To put it all in perspective, there is quite a difference between creating the big idea and stopping the big problem.

When we excel at finding new ways to screw up, our clients never experience the problem.

Our goal in DevOps is to make things simple. Flawless.

In the creative world, our best ideas win awards, wow customers, and get us all excited.

Our message is as simple as great DevOps.

Take the time to make things simple.

If you are not sure your apps are being built with this proficiency, your instinct is probably right. Ask and find out.

If your in-house team tells you everything is fine, ask how they find new ways to screw up and have them explain it to you.

If the mindset and skills are there, you will have far fewer issues than most firms.

If you are crossing your fingers because that "other group" handles your new apps, well, we will cross our fingers for you that your luck continues.

In an increasingly software-driven world, our team who finds new ways to screw up is more important than ever.

Since that is not such a catchy name, we'll just keep calling them DevOps.

LEADERSHIP INSIGHT

What Are Your Triggers?

We all know that when certain things happen, we can be triggered. We get defensive, sometimes emotional, and don't think straight.

A trigger occurs because we are sensitized to behavior due to our past, in most cases.

And it is usually the wrong reaction and a waste of time.

You can't stop your brain or your memories from kicking in.

What you can do is to be honest with yourself about what your triggers are, and when you recognize them kicking in, you do your best to recognize it and get to normal as quickly as you can.

It is hard work for all of us. Just talk about it and embrace it. It's normal.

CHAPTER 62

HOW HUMANS LEARN BEST

"The world is a book and those
who do not travel read only one page."
—*Saint Augustine*

There is a reason why I have flown more than five million miles and have stayed in hotels for more than one thousand nights in my career.

You build the best relationships when you get to know someone in person.

You create the most impactful ideas when you can whiteboard a potential solution together.

You understand the team dynamics of a group you either manage or consult with by observing them in their normal environment.

You can learn from your peers in minutes with a quick question or by peering over their shoulder.

We are built to take a wide range of social cues from all our interactions and either store them for future use or act on them in the moment.

You can't do this via Zoom or Teams.

The good news is this has nothing to do with being remote. Leaders who are remote are just as capable of visiting clients, using a whiteboard, and creating times where they can teach their team new ideas and ways to work in incremental steps.

In fact, I would argue that some people who live close to headquarters and visit the office often do less of this. Some of us choose not to interact as much with our peers or take the time to visit with clients and partners of all types.

Now, if we do get back to the office setting, it's important to remember what we can accomplish by being together. To let this sink in further, think of your world for a few minutes.

When you present in person, you can read the room and see who is loving what you say, who may have a contrary view, and who is tuned out.

When you whiteboard, you can visualize a concept, talk about it, and invite your peers to add to the visual.

When you are working on a new spreadsheet to analyze a business outcome, you can lean over and ask if your neighbor can take a look and let you know if you are on track.

You can meet for a meal with your team or clients and see how they ask questions, understand what issues they are dealing with, and learn more about people on a personal basis.

The best consultants and team leaders realize that this time is actually the most important time they spend each and every day. You can inspire, teach, and map out solutions that may have just sat in your head otherwise.

The epiphany, at least for me, is that being productive is relative.

The power of the crowd helps us all make better decisions.

The question is, who is your crowd? Once you know that, you can choose how to inspire and benefit that crowd?

CHAPTER 63

ONE BIG DIFFERENCE BETWEEN MANAGERS AND LEADERS—THE +4 MODEL

"Before you are a leader, success is all about growing yourself. When you become a leader, success is all about growing others."

—*Jack Welch*

Some consultants dread more work. How will they get it all done? Can they really take on more work? Doesn't anyone realize they are already working as hard as they can? I mean...come on!

It all sounds logical, but these are the wrong questions to ask.

Leaders who learn to scale businesses ask a different set of questions:

Who can I hire who is better than me in a certain area?

How can I eventually hire four leaders who are better than me?

Are those leaders building out their own teams and doing the same thing?

It's what we call the +4 model. It's how leaders scale and is critical to your success.

Find the four people who unlock your potential. If you don't, you'll never witness what you are capable of accomplishing.

So, why is it so hard for some of us to do this? Well, here are the types of management styles that get in the way:

I'm the only one who can do this. You may be smart and efficient at what you do, but even if you were building a rocket to go to Mars, there are other people who can do the same work. So, maybe, just perhaps, there is someone else who can also write press releases or build a media plan.

I don't have time to figure this out, don't you get it? The difference between a manager and a leader is the latter understands they need to take a breath, think about the future, and build their team strategically. If they don't, the work drives them, and they complain they are on a hamster wheel.

I hired one of my +4s, but I don't trust their work. Instead of taking time to help the new leader understand what to do, we just assume they will do it just like us. You must invest in your reports to help them be their best. It doesn't happen via a magic wand.

Clients really want me. We think the client cannot live without us. In reality, our client expects us to build an effective team.

This is one of the big differences between managing and leading.

A manager works hard every day, but seldom thinks too far ahead.

A leader also works hard every day, but realizes a strong team is always smarter, better, and more likely to succeed than an individual superstar. They are continually nurturing the growth of their team, meeting new people who may join, and embracing the creation of a strong team.

Another way to look at it is individual superstars remain the star of their small pond. Leaders develop, scale, and build what's next in the open seas of consulting.

The question is, who do you want to be? And what steps are you taking to get there?

Not everyone wants to scale. If you are one of them, embrace it and don't give your team a hard time for not being you.

If you do follow the +4, you'll be pleasantly surprised at what you can build over the years.

And remember, growth and the work itself should be fun…most of the time.

CHAPTER 64

THE FUTURE OF THE WORKPLACE

"Nothing will work unless you do."

—*Maya Angelou*

My first consulting job was in 1985, and we were talking about the future of the workplace.

It's a topic that is always top of mind.

The famous behaviorist, Kurt Lewin, built a model that describes a three-step process for achieving personal and organizational change. The first stage—unfreezing—involves recognizing that change is necessary, so we need to dismantle old beliefs and practices. Change occurs in the second stage and is often accompanied by confusion and distress as the old mindset or system breaks down. The third and final stage—freezing—occurs when a new mindset is crystallized and there is an accompanying sense of comfort and stability within the new framework.

The process involves painful unlearning, difficult relearning, and restructuring thoughts, feelings, attitudes, and perceptions.

It's something we have been doing as long as offices existed.

It brings Covid-19 to mind because it was such a wrenching change in our work environment. We had never seen such a disruption since World War II, which was arguably far more impactful.

Thinking about how big societal changes have impacted the workplace,

I'm, ironically, reminded about how common the issues have always been. After all, humans haven't changed.

As far back as I can remember, the most successful people figured out how to get out of the office to meet with clients, identify new opportunities, and find time to work in the office to support their teams, create innovative ideas, and share their learnings.

It is this "hybrid osmosis" that works so well. We learn from the adventurers who travel far and wide. We need to learn from each other in person, since we do it so much easier and are more likely to pick up important signals from our clients and our team by seeing them in person. We can notice micro expressions, see team dynamics, and understand how we can make an impact.

Of course, we are perpetually unsatisfied with the status quo of work, so we experiment.

The advent of technology in the '90s started to make it possible for the "office" to include one's home office. It was the technology industry, long before Covid-19, that started experimenting with how workers could work from home and how much of their work could be done in countries far away, the ultimate in remote work.

This experiment, which is now over thirty years old, has led to a hybrid environment, where workers who really don't need to be with customers or build and manage teams can work remotely, but leaders now need to learn how to become proficient at interacting with clients and their teams in person and via streaming video.

New times require new skills. They also remind us we are best when we are directly with our teams and our clients, so how we spend our time matters more than ever.

Covid-19 has just forced us to rethink how we work. You could say it resulted in "unfreezing" the "we have to be here five days a week" mentality. The length of Covid-19 was long enough that we then "froze" new behaviors that also need to be thawed out, like the idea that "anyone can work from home now."

The debate will continue. Thirty years from now, I am confident you will be arguing about what the right mix of work is and why you are right.

What is important to reflect on is what has always been important and what will continue to be important because we are human beings. Our tendencies are easy to figure out. We match that up with the realities of our customers and clients, and we have some strong guidelines to consider for the future of the workplace.

Here is a way to consider framing your discussion, wherever you work:

#1 – Will my work choices increase value for our clients/customers? How are you creating more value, and how are you unlocking the value of the firm overall?

#2 – If I am a manager, will my work choices accelerate my team's career development? How am I improving how I manage my team, and would they agree the way we work is better this way?

#3 – How often will I see my clients/partners/agencies in person to build the best relationship? How often do I meet someone for breakfast? Visit a client in person? Host people at our firm? Attend conferences? Am I building a strong future network?

#4 – How will I create new ideas and whiteboard our future? The most effective innovators acknowledge great ideas come from brainstorming and whiteboarding with a team. How are you doing it?

#5 – Is each leader making the right decision on their workflow to improve our firm? If your leader was here right now, would their case for their workflow choice prompt you to say, "Wow! This is well thought through and provides the most value for the firm and the leader"? Or would you say, "Oh, this is just about their needs, not ours."

What we cannot escape is we are choosing to work in the organization we are in. We have an obligation to use our presence to make it more valuable. If we don't share that philosophy, we're in the wrong place.

The punchline is there is no right answer. What we do know is the extremes are not necessary. You don't have to be at the office five days a week from nine to five. And you should not be at home every day of the week. Neither is productive long term.

The hybrid workplace has always existed.

The best way to envision it, in my view, is to remember why great leaders were so successful.

They visit clients regularly, or if a client, they visit their partners regularly.

They dream up new ideas in person and create a culture of innovation as a result.

They can pick up the signals from their team and serve as great mentors.

They unlock value via personal contact, but also love their time at home or in an office with headphones on, where they can write, plan, and catch up. They were never in the office five days a week.

They have figured out how to unlock their value, and everyone agrees.

As a side note, there will be people working remote who will say they have to work remote, so this doesn't fit. That's not true. Here are a few ways to help you think about it differently:

Why not recruit other people locally to your firm and start a mini office?

How can you turn your streaming sessions into your own "office"? How can you nurture careers, speak for minutes, not hours, and brainstorm with your team via streaming? This will only improve as an option in the years ahead. Help us innovate the remote experience.

Show us how to make high-quality office visits with your team.

Lead us by visiting your clients, in person, on a regular basis. You can visit and network from anywhere.

The key is to accept what works, deal with our own situations, and then make the most of them.

Human beings will always prefer to interact in person. The way our brains are wired is not about to change.

It is about how we rework and rewire how we spend our time, so we make the most impact in any hybrid situation.

Make the most of how you can provide value, and you will do great. Don't get defensive.

Help us create a future workplace that will be special.

Meanwhile, I am confident we will engage in the never-ending discussion on the future of the workplace.

CHAPTER 65

THE GAME OF TIME

"Ordinary people think merely of spending time,
great people think of using it."
—*Arthur Schopenhauer*

Time is our most important asset, and it is the one that continually disappears.

We tend to look at the historical analysis of time and complain, usually about its use.

It happens for a simple reason.

We spend far too much time analyzing how people *spent* their time. We spend far too little time determining how people should *use* their time in the future.

To understand how to use time effectively, we need to start with how we screw it up. If you are looking not to do this well, here are your tips for the day:

> *Focus on billability. Talk about whether someone is 75 or 85 percent billable and make dramatic and emotional statements about their work. Don't address billing rates or take the time to know if these hours will all get billed to the client. Just obsess over the percentage, and you can ensure you will never make any real progress.*
>
> *Celebrate people with great billability, but don't challenge the formula used to generate their billability. Don't allow team members to include*

training or internal meetings, so their billable percentage continues to shine.

Only look at the most recent month and draw conclusions.

There's more, but you get the point.

We are allowing the game of time to game us.

There is a better way, and it is deceptively simple, as are all great models.

Here are four ingredients to understand how we most effectively use time:

#1 – Focus on annual hours billed to a client. We set a goal at the beginning of the year and then measure against the actual hours billed to a client. We may say the goal is 1500 hours and look at our progress towards that goal throughout the year. Create a goal for each title and each person. Just like how we look at revenue and profit. Same exact approach.

#2 – Adjust targets based on total value. If any team member receives a reduced annual goal, it is because we expect them to offset these hours via growth (organic and new business) that will clearly outweigh this "give back." ROI can now be measured for each leader with reduced hourly goals.

#3 – Understand a team's value and our pricing. We can now look at each team member and do simple math. Their total hours for the year billed to clients multiplied by their hourly rate equals a total revenue number per person *(total hours billed x hourly rate = realized revenue)*. Now, when you look at a spreadsheet of your team's progress, you can see who needs more client work and who may be working too much for their level, and you can redistribute workflow. It is normal to realize we aren't staffed as efficiently as we could be, and our pricing isn't reflective of our total value.

#4 – Continually address your use of contractors. If we are using contractors because they have skills we don't have and never want to have, then we are making a smart choice. If we are using contractors as a way to avoid making a key hire (postponement), then we are very likely wasting resources. Our total revenue billed via contractors should be tracked, so we can see when/if we can hire and decrease our total. Think of it as "lost revenue" and reconfirm throughout the year that you are only utilizing talent you absolutely cannot access via other means.

This approach ensures our team members can take time off and engage in other activities inside or outside the firm, as long as they hit their numbers for the year. It enables us to see what our productivity is per person and measure improvement over the years (e.g., revenue per person). And we can see how to redistribute workflow by title, as well as recalibrate our pricing to match up with the demand on our most precious resource—our time.

In embracing a more strategic view of time, we learn how to "use it" and avoid the whiplash that can occur when billability goes up and down throughout the year. As important, we learn to value ourselves more and ensure we are staffing optimally, pricing correctly, and hiring the team we deserve.

Stay the course. Be strategic. Focus on the game of time, but don't let it game you.

LEADERSHIP INSIGHT

Slowness of a Moment

When a serious moment occurs, like a crisis, some of us actually feel like the world is slowing down. We have an ability to adjust and stay calm when we know what is hitting the fan.

How do you achieve this state if it isn't natural for you?

The best way is to realize the competition for Zen is noise. And that noise is in your head.

If you are well-read on the client's business, well-practiced in the issues that will be faced, and are used to being in the same room with senior leaders, the next issue is not that big a deal, at least emotionally.

That is a long way to say that it takes practice.

If you were a baseball player and asked how not to get nervous with the bases loaded, two outs, and the game is tied in the bottom of the ninth, the real answer is you have to be in that situation many times before it becomes routine.

Practice, study, be prepared, and trust yourself. After all, your client is counting on you.

CHAPTER 66

THE INGREDIENTS OF A LEADING TEAM

"The main ingredient of stardom is the rest of the team."

—John Wooden

John Wooden won ten NCAA basketball championships in twelve years and is considered one of the most humble and successful sports coaches of all time.

We know that Coach Wooden believed in the power of the entire team. But what was his genius? In my view, it was his ability to understand all the ingredients he had to work with (his players, coaching staff, their game plans, and the potential of each player), and then he crafted solutions. He wasn't just lucky. He was truly an expert at seeing what he had to work with and making the most of it. This concept applies to us whether we are building our teams or assessing how we embrace technology. It is a thinking process that helps us evolve.

We believe that every team reflects how well they have identified and put together the ingredients that can lead to success. They are sometimes obvious, such as skill, experience, industry expertise, management ability, and creativity, and then there are the X factors, which can include our ability to use technology in our work, who we choose to work with, our ability to think ahead, and other tangibles.

That kind of sounds true but also like mumbo-jumbo to a degree. We recommend avoiding diving right into management 101 and, instead, forcing ourselves to think outside our normal pattern.

As you read this, your phone is probably right next to you, so let us start with this device and then the supporting network that makes it all possible.

With the iPhone, we can quickly agree it is a computer, a music library, a camera, and a cellphone. It has an app store that enables anyone in the world to access us.

It has computer chips for quick action and memory. Megapixel technology for the camera.

Easy. We know all that. What we spend less time on is thinking about how the browser works or how email services are integrated or how data is leveraged. And we spend even less time learning about the top five metals used in an iPhone—aluminum, iron, lithium, gold, and copper. Where do they come from? How is it made? Or how is it priced?

We tend to focus on the surface and not dig deep into all the ingredients necessary for success.

Of course, none of these cool things can be done on an iPhone without a global technology infrastructure. So, now let's think about the enterprise data center, which includes routers, switches, firewalls, storage systems, servers, and application delivery controllers.

These ingredients store and manage data and applications, provide security, connect servers (physical and virtual), and provide processing, memory, storage, and network connectivity. They make it easy for us to access whatever we want, wherever we are.

And here is the lesson for us when building great teams:

You want the best people to work at your organization, but you must surround them with the right technology, right data sources, right external partners, and so on.

As the leader of your team, you need to ask yourself questions that can help everyone improve, such as:

Are we using technology in the optimal way? What does that even mean?

Are we accessing the right data sources, and do we have the right training to gain insights?

How do our team members get smarter throughout the year?

When did we last brief our agency or our client on what's next?

How exactly are we improving recruiting, so we access the best talent each time?

It is a lengthy list, and one you don't finish in a meeting or a quarter or even a year. It is a way of thinking that makes us remember that if you don't have enough aluminum, you ain't making an iPhone, and if you don't protect your data, it could be hacked.

The key when identifying ingredients for success is to remember that we (the humans) are part of it and so is the technology we choose to use and the knowledge we access.

When we spend our time staring at organization charts for too long, I believe we get dumber. When you find yourself in big groups that aren't getting anything done, or you're staring at information but aren't sure what to do next, remember that every minute of this time could be spent analyzing how to integrate technology into your workflow, coaching a team member on how to innovate, or finding some other way to unlock your team and yourself. Minimize time spent on bureaucracy. Coach Wooden wasn't known for long staff meetings or side meetings on what type of uniform his team should wear. He focused on his players, the plays they would run, and how they would win more than most coaches in the league. The results speak for themselves.

The headline is simple. People are critical to building a consulting team. People with the right access to other smart people and the right data and technology are the ones who will lead the way.

Coach Wooden's teams were known for being in phenomenal physical shape, since they practiced more intensely than their peers. Often, towards the end of the game, they would pull out a win due to their skill and preparation.

For all leaders reading this book, that's our question. Are we preparing like Coach Wooden? Or are we preparing like the teams that were pretty good, but that UCLA routinely beat?

Every day, we can make the choice to dig into the details and never be satisfied with the status quo.

CHAPTER 67

THE UNOFFICIAL RULES OF PARTNERING WITH A PRIME

"Collaboration equals innovation."

—*Michael Dell*

When building a firm, we will often look for ways to partner with a larger organization, which is referred to as a "prime" or lead partner. We want to build strong relationships with third-party organizations, who can open doors for us and expand their relationship to include us as a sub-contractor. Over the years, the unofficial rules of partnering with a prime have become clear.

If you are the sub-contractor or even just a co-partner, how you decide to show up matters.

When you are a "sub," you are being invited into the "house" of the "prime." Similar to visiting a new friend today, you would walk into the house, be polite, and follow the advice of your new friend inside their house. You would not walk in the house, go upstairs, take a nap, then fire up the grill, find a steak in the fridge, and start cooking. It's common sense.

Here's our guide:

#1 – Relationship – Understand the relationship between the prime and the client. Is this an initial or long-standing relationship? What type of pricing will work? What type of leverage does each partner have? Who leads the business on both sides and why? What is our role in the relationship? Is the partner aligned with our thinking?

#2 – Status – Define if this is a "white label" or a "known brand" relationship. Does the partner prefer to only discuss and use their brand when we work, or is it ok for us to use our own brand when working with our client?

#3 – Alignment – What is our partner's project timeline? Do we have clarity on the timing and expectations for our deliverables?

#4 – Access – Does our partner expect us to speak with the client direct and/or separately? If so, determine the shared agenda and expected outcome prior to the meeting. Rule of thumb is a sub talks with the client if the client makes an unsolicited request and the partner agrees.

#5 – Future – Do we pursue our own business flow outside of this partnership? It is expected that we complete the assignment before discussing a separate MSA or any side projects unless there is express permission from the partner.

Essentially, staying aligned with the partner so the partner's relationship is successful leads to more business. Partners who view subs as getting ahead of the relationship are rarely asked back for future opportunities. In summary, we think of this situation as having to satisfy two clients, both the actual client and the prime.

CHAPTER 68

WHAT ARE WE CHOOSING NOT TO DO?

"Those people who are crazy enough to think they can change the world are the ones that actually do."

—*Steve Jobs*

There are many famous stories of a CEO hesitating and losing momentum, no matter how successful they were previously.

Some involve risk avoidance. Intel CEO Paul Otellini passed on Steve Jobs' offer (2005) to start making chips for the iPhone. Turns out, Jobs' forecast was off. It was about 100x greater, but Otellini was more concerned with the hit to profit margin at the time.

Some involve a lack of imagination. Why didn't Blockbuster evolve into Netflix?

Some involve too much confidence. How could cars made outside the US ever crack the market?

It sure is easy to look backward and critique, but that's not worth much. Every decision to move forward (or not) was surely a tough one to make. For there are just as many failures for moving forward at the wrong time as there are successes for taking the right gamble.

I have a lot of compassion for the leaders who didn't move at the right time and remember that most of them also made quite a few successful moves, which is why they were in the position to make this call.

So, back to us. I have found the best question to ask yourself is, "What are we choosing not to do?"

Each year, you make a conscious choice about what to invest time and resources in and make an equal decision about what you will not do. We spend most, if not all, our time on the former, outlining our priorities for the year, developing key performance indicators, and measuring our success throughout the year.

We do not spend enough time outlining what we won't do, yet it is important.

In my experience, leaders of successful firms have their equivalent of a "3x3" plan in their heads at all times. They know the plan for next year and are already thinking of their important moves for year two and year three. In fact, much of their work in year one will help set up years two and three.

The key point, however, is that they speak the most about the current year, since they want to ensure the firm is focused on the present.

A leadership team needs to walk and chew gum. Focus intently on year one, while continually discussing how the firm will evolve in year two and three. This will involve bringing in new types of talent, opening new offices, developing new practices, firms you may invest in, awards you want to win, changes in your workplace, and more.

In talking actively at the leadership team level, e.g., your executive council, you ensure leaders are aligned on the overall vision and, more importantly, have their eyes and ears open to identify opportunities whenever they present themselves.

Most of us will make a series of decisions that incrementally grow our firms.

If we wait until we are ready to make a call, our risk level will actually increase, since we have not had the benefit of continually thinking about the future.

To use a simple analogy, think about talent.

If you have identified the perfect #2 for one of your top leaders and imagine them joining your firm in year two, this is part of a good plan. But then you meet this person the next week and realize they fit the profile perfectly.

Do you try to keep in touch for a year and hope they are available? (Not likely.) Or do you bite the bullet and hire them now?

We often hear luck happens to those who prepare, or we are told about the amazing gut instinct of a certain entrepreneur. In reality, leaders who are super prepared and always think ahead several years are ready when an opportunity arises. On the flip side, if you're too focused on the present and are blocking out the future, those same opportunities will pass you by, and you will never know it.

Yes, this approach can impact margins in the short term. And sometimes your decisions won't work.

In the long run, however, you have significantly increased your ability to grow your firm.

Let's end with another brief exercise.

List the decisions you are not making this year, ask if any of them would add value, then question why you are saying no. Now, ask yourself if you are postponing the decision due to risk, lack of imagination, or confidence. Be as honest with yourself as you are capable.

Here are how a few items on this list could look:

1. **Hire a practice leader for consumer marketing (risk).** Salary requirements are too high, and we are not sure of first-year revenue growth.
2. **Build PESO (paid, earned, shared, and owned) media function (lack of imagination).** Not sure if we know how to weave together paid, earned, shared, and owned media into one team. Table for now.
3. **Open London office (confidence).** What if we don't succeed? What will the marketplace think of us?

The list starts to look familiar. And what you realize quickly is that the obstacle to moving forward is more often between your ears.

Talk aloud to your leadership team. Chart a path to break out of what is comfortable and make choices that will advance the firm. And remember, if you fail now and then, so what. That's part of life, personally and professionally.

CHAPTER 69

WHY INTEGRATION IS A NO-NO AND OTHER WORDS TO AVOID

"Yesterday is but today's memory and tomorrow is today's dream."

—*Khalil Gibran*

It is the words of a Lebanese-American poet, writer, and visual artist, Khalil Gibran, who captures an important point about how we deal with the past and create the future with our clients.

Words are powerful because of the associations they create in our minds and our memories.

In our business, we use words, phrases, and experiences to build a powerful narrative and create new memories that will be long lasting.

Like a great editor, we should provide equal care to what we don't share.

Here is why:

- Every client we meet with has a history, positive and negative, with firms like ours.
- They remember the events in their lives that matter to them.
- They walk into our conference room with this basket of experiences.
- Then, our brains kick in, which are really the first search engines ever created.

When we use Google, we write and speak a few words to a machine, and it searches for us to find relevant information.

Our brains do the same thing. We hear a word, phrase, or experience, and our minds start searching for relevancy in our past.

If our past experience was a good one, wonderful. If it wasn't, our minds can't help but fill with the details of that outcome.

As a result, we can create "noise" that triggers bad memories without knowing it, if we are not careful.

Now, imagine words as a laser pointer showing us where to go.

Words can remind us of a memory. Associate us with a certain outcome. Direct us to a new way to think.

We may tell a client about a person we know in common. Or we mention a campaign we completed that is directly applicable to their needs. Or we may discuss a new model for the first time.

We can also trigger a bad experience with the use of a simple word.

"Integration" is a great example. It's jargon for "we work together well."

But when you have to say you do something that should be routine, you are trying too hard, just like all the other firms the client remembers.

It's kind of like a hospital saying, "We are clean on every floor!" Well, I sure hope so.

When we realize that the words we use trigger memories in the minds of those we are speaking to, we start to choose our words with far more precision.

If we remember that our choice of words, phrases, references, and stories all provide direction, then we can think through what we share with more care. Here are a few examples:

The trigger word with no credibility—This is like playing corporate bingo. We start saying, "We didn't have the bandwidth, so we had to pivot, but we're now fully integrated and working towards the new normal. Of course, we can take it offline to discuss more." When you use these words, you are telling the listener you don't know what you're saying. You are coming across like someone lost in corporate gobbledygook.

The redirect word or phrase – We may be ready to discuss an important public relations program, but we can't resist talking about an exciting new initiative we are doing in advertising that has nothing to do with our plan that day. Our minds drift toward the discipline of advertising rather than prepare for more information in public relations.

Random mentions of past places and people – If you haven't done your homework, you mention a firm or a person that was not a great relationship for your client. Now, they are thinking of their negative experience while judging you.

The distracting comment – You are ready to discuss a serious new initiative, but you can't resist sharing that you love to juggle in Bryant Park at night. Nothing wrong with juggling, but share it in context and at the right time. Not right before a more serious conversation.

What we can do about this is straight forward. Talk about which words you commonly use that are trigger words and avoid them—integration, reengineering, etc.

Realize you have an awesome tool to use—your choice of words, phrases, and experiences.

Eliminate jargon from your speech or make fun of it.

Redirect to new topics that are inspiring with purpose.

Share examples from the past that will strengthen your relationship and illustrate why you are the right choice.

Save the really personal stuff for your friends, family, and colleagues at work.

Create tomorrow's dream with today's words.

LEADERSHIP INSIGHT

A Full Perspective on Compensation Discussions with Leaders

It is review season, and your top leaders want more compensation. Lots of it.

Time for perspective as you look to reward them.

How will you increase your pricing as you raise compensation costs?

What costs can be avoided or decreased, so you maintain the same or better profit margin?

What will the leader do differently next year to align with their compensation ask?

As long as a firm continues to remain profitable and continues to grow due to the leader's efforts, these are easy conversations. They are not when leaders want more compensation, but don't have ideas on how to raise revenue and reduce costs to pay for their efforts. After all, it is a business we all help run together.

Share the full perspective, and you will get full buy-in. We all want to get it right.

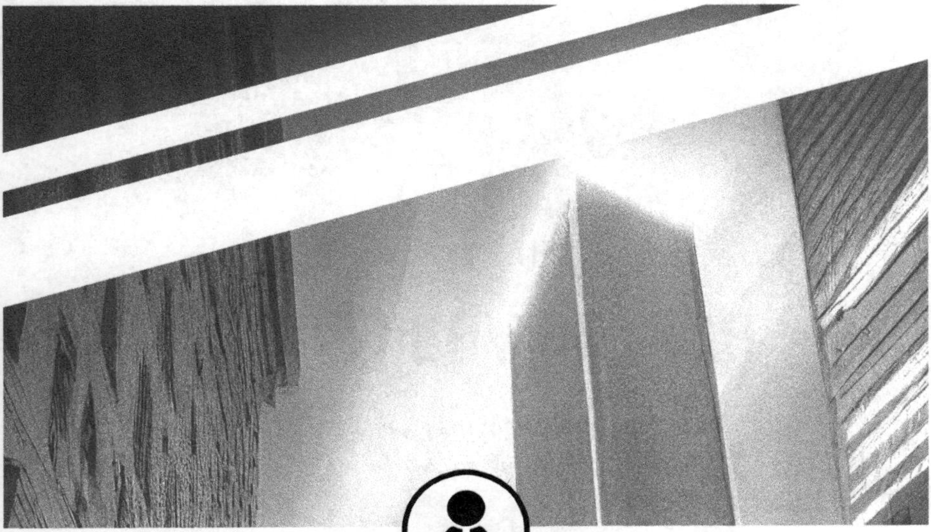

PERSONAL GROWTH

CHAPTER 70

HOW DO YOU LEARN?

"The noblest pleasure is the joy of understanding."

—Leonardo da Vinci

Leaders who are eager to improve how they work realize they need to *change* how they learn.

It often leads to the question, "How do I learn, and what do I need to do?"

My view is that there is no magic bullet. Rather, what we all need is an intellectual regimen to follow if we choose to steadily increase our knowledge base. Kind of like a physical workout. We're just focusing on our brain in this case.

To illustrate this point, I will share the five key areas of learning I have found helpful, along with examples from my current regimen.

FIVE KEY AREAS OF LEARNING

#1—Read outside of your normal zone. Take time to read materials that count as "learning," not entertainment. It may be more school-like, and the books or studies may not be "fun," but they are important. Right now, I am focusing on anything related to China, space, and rare earth minerals, like cobalt.

#2—Go deep on innovative technologies so you understand just enough. You don't have to get a physics or electrical engineering degree, but you should spend time understanding the basics of technology. For the next few years, I am focusing more on qubit (quantum computing), 6G (next generation after 5G cellular networks), the rise of audio (50 percent of search is already verbal), the future of likeness (think digital avatars), and new search engines, like Shodan (tracks IOT devices). It looks like a random list, but each technology plays a key role in our future. Someday it will make a lot more sense.

#3 – Pick a topic each year and learn about it. This year, it is cybersecurity. I read *The Cuckoo's Egg*, *Sandworm*, a bunch of Kevin Mitnick's books, and regularly peruse Brian Krebs' newsletter. Next year, it will be something else.

#4 – Imagine that all innovative ideas will not occur in my "world." Keep track of interesting conferences worldwide. Learn about how innovation is occurring in a region of the world you don't know as well. Imagine that most innovation will not occur right in front of you. I find it fascinating to keep up with innovation in Asia, but also keep an eye on Africa and regions like the Baltics. You never know where the next ideas will come from.

#5 – Spend time thinking like the audience we want to reach. What is it like to have a rare disease? Maybe you read a biography. What is it like to build autonomous vehicles? Why was Greenpeace created, and how are movements started? I am reading a biography on Elon Musk and a book about how Greenpeace started next.

Yes, it's a real commitment to build your knowledge base.

Now, step out of this mindset and imagine a leader you know who seems to effortlessly shift topics with any client and adds value. Why is that?

I will make the argument that for most of us, the ability to pivot in conversation and discuss such a wide range of topics is due to a commitment to learning in ways that are different than one's peers, who usually read the exact same thing their peers read.

Think about what you read every day. Ask yourself if every competitor is reading the exact same information you are reading. If yes, you risk falling behind.

Create your own learning regimen and put in the hard work to broaden your intellectual base.

The ball is in your court.

CHAPTER 71

HOW TO TURN NEGATIVE FEEDBACK INTO NEW OPPORTUNITIES

"Every problem is an opportunity in disguise."

—*John Adams*

When I was in sales calling on physicians, pharmacies, and hospitals, I learned to say that every problem is just a speed bump on the road to success.

What I learned at an early age was how powerful it can be to listen to those who are upset, help diagnose their problem, and then solve it.

It is hard to do. We often get triggered when people present us with their problems. We are dismissive sometimes, which really just protects our ego. Or we just say they are nuts, another way to dismiss.

There is another way. It's hard to do, but it sure does work.

Here are three examples from when I was "carrying the bag" as a sales rep:

The Story of Actigall

Actigall was a drug that helped dissolve gallstones. For some people, it was an alternative to surgery.

Well, I walked into one office in the south of my territory to meet two physicians for the first time. I was excited to meet them and introduce myself.

That lasted for about five seconds.

As soon as they realized which company and product I represented, they lit into me. I heard all their complaints at once. They were ignored. They didn't get samples. They didn't receive medical literature they asked for. They just had "had it" with our company and this treatment due to our lack of attention.

I listened, acknowledged their concerns, and said, "Thank you. That means a lot to me that you would tell me exactly what we did wrong. I agree with you, and I am going to show you that times are different...if you will give me a chance."

They had expected me to argue. Instead, I agreed they were right. And then I did everything they asked for.

They turned out to be one of our higher volume offices.

My Cardiologist Counselor

Specialty doctors are very difficult to see. If you get in, you need to remember that they are super smart and have zero time.

I walked into the office of one of the top cardiologists in my territory and was given a quick moment. The doctor proceeded to tell me he was tired of being told what to do, didn't believe in the marketing crap he would get served, and didn't really have time to see reps like me.

It was immediately clear that I would never get a chance to go through the carefully curated sales aid flow sent to me by headquarters. That was clearly out the window. I could also see that this doctor was also right. Why would he waste time hearing sales pitches in between doing important cardiovascular procedures? Yet, we had treatments we know he used and needed to keep up on.

So, what do you do?

I pivoted. I said, "Dr. X, that makes sense. Here is my ask. I just received new sales materials from headquarters, and my job is to explain what matters to GPs (general practitioners) and IMs (internal medicine). Could you look at what I received and tell me what you believe I should focus on?"

Now, it was an intellectual challenge. This cardiologist could spend a few minutes to teach me, so I can reach his referral network with the best messaging.

He took the materials, looked them over, and proceeded to explain what I should focus on.

I said, "Thank you. This is what I will do, appreciate your time." Then, I started to pack up to leave, and the doctor interrupted me to say, "Make sure you get your samples to our team." For those who don't know pharma sales, samples are how you start new patients with a free week or month of treatment.

And that was our new relationship. Infrequent, but highly focused meetings that were productive for both of us.

Work Ethic

I often ran into other sales reps who all knew each other from years of working the same territory. I heard them bragging about how they only worked ten to three or nine to four, and I realized they were doing enough to do well, but not more.

What an opportunity!

I started working earlier and ending later. When doctor's offices closed, I would go see a few pharmacists and listen to them. The unmet need here was the simplest. If I just worked harder, I would see more doctors and increase the universe I could reach versus the average rep who was seeing the core group. Widen the universe, and you expand your sales. Just through more effort. Too easy!

What I have learned can be summarized into four key insights:

#1 – Always solve the unmet needs of your customer, not yours. Be relentless about finding the underlying cause of what they care about the most and then solve the problem.

#2 – Never get triggered; listen, then do the right thing. Don't get triggered when you want to react, keep listening, and then focus on the right next steps. And if you do get triggered, remind yourself that this just hurt you. Keep trying.

#3 – Ask your best clients to teach you now and then. You collaborate with smart people. Make it a two-way street, which is far more interesting for smart clients. They want a learning dialogue, not a one-way relationship.

#4 – When you work harder, you uncover new opportunities. Working more hours expanded my universe of doctors, helping me develop relationships my competitors didn't have.

Problems start out feeling like "uh oh" moments, but they often become "aha" opportunities you can uniquely solve.

CHAPTER 72

THE IMPORTANCE OF MANAGING YOUR EMOTIONS

"You will continue to suffer if you have an emotional reaction to everything that is said to you. True power is sitting back and observing things with logic. True power is restraint. If words control you that means everyone else can control you. Breathe and allow things to pass."

— *anonymous*

We all know the settings.

A leader yells at us and sets us off. All we can think about is how unfair this is or how wrong they are.

A team member calls us to complain about a colleague. Lots of emotion, few facts. We listen and start to get upset about the situation.

Someone doesn't do exactly what we thought they would do, and we get irritated.

Every time this happens, we are letting emotion cloud our brain.

When our brains are cloudy, so is our thinking.

As a leader, it is very hard to control our thoughts sometimes, but everyone is depending on us to do so.

Here are key learnings I have accumulated from doing this well and, quite frankly, from doing it poorly:

#1 – Focus on the facts. Do your best to separate emotion from fact. Both are important and relevant. Just understand which one you are dealing with more.

#2 – Remember this is not cancer, just an issue. It is interesting to remember that when truly serious issues arise, we get more focused and non-emotional, so we can figure out what to do. I can say this first-hand as a cancer survivor (prostate). Don't let other people's emotional state become yours.

#3 – Take time to respond, don't rush. We often have our best ideas for business when we let the problem percolate for a day or more. Think fast, act slow. Give it time.

#4 – Teach your colleagues how to respond as well. Teach your team how to present you with a problem. Often, it is fair to ask a person to provide you an update on the problem and a recommended solution. Too often, we are presented with a problem without any thought of the solution. A straightforward way to ask this is, "What would you do if you were in my shoes?"

The best leaders are known for being unflappable. The bigger the issue, the calmer they are. It's often the mark, in fact, of those of us who excel in crisis/issues support for companies.

When I look back on my career, I remember situations where I was triggered and reacted emotionally.

I can say that I wish I did not do that in 100 percent of the cases. I am even more proud of the many more times I have listened, learned, and partnered with leaders to figure out what to do next.

Remember that everything you do as a leader sends a message. Be in control and send the message you want to send, not the one others try to force out of you.

LEADERSHIP INSIGHT

My North Star— The Best Advice I Ever Received

When I played baseball, one of the other players on our high school team was Mike Loynd, who went on to win the Golden Spikes Award for best player in college (Florida State) and then had a brief career in the major leagues. Since my dad was our coach, he got to know Mike's Dad, Dick Loynd, who had a tremendous business career that included serving as CEO of Converse.

Dick offered to meet with me once I started working, so at the age of twenty-three, I visited Mr. Loynd at his office and asked him the questions that were on my mind. I remember his answers, but one, in particular, stood out.

"What is the most important thing I can do to improve my career?"

He said, "Bobby, your reputation is the most important thing you will ever have in your life. No one else but you will guard it and respect it. Just remember that in the years ahead."

I was expecting he would tell me to read more or get my MBA earlier or something else. This seemed so esoteric. But as it sunk in, I realized he had just given me my North Star.

Years later, our daughter Brittany was sitting in class at Texas Christian University. The professor asked the students what the best advice they have ever received was. Brittany wrote what I just shared above. Brittany was captain of her cheerleading team that won two national championships and had witnessed and given inspirational talks of her own. Yet, this is what resonated.

(continues on the next page)

(continued from the previous page)

It's true. No matter what happens in life, the one thing you take with you is your reputation.

It is something I reflect on during those moments when no one is looking.

Am I proud of what I am doing? Am I guarding and respecting my own reputation?

We could argue that our confidence in life is directly tied to how we view ourselves. And the more confident we are in who we are, the more likely we are to consistently do the right thing.

CHAPTER 73

THE SMALL POND SYNDROME

"What we fear of doing most is usually what we most need to do."

—Ralph Waldo Emerson

The original "Waldo," an American essayist, said it best.

We fear change. We fear taking risk.

We feel comfortable doing what we have done before with people we trust and with outcomes we can predict.

Nothing wrong with that, but when you are in growth mode, you need to continually ask yourself if you are resisting growth and not being honest with yourself about why you are resisting.

Small pond syndrome might as well be called the "entrepreneur's dilemma."

You have built a strong offering. You have hired people you trust. You are getting results. And you have steady revenue.

But you want to be five or ten times as large. You know you can do it. You say you want to do it, but you don't, and you get increasingly irritated that you aren't succeeding.

The small pond syndrome deserves a look in the mirror. Here is what you often see:

No one can follow you up the mountain. Leaders who scale have a +4 team, which means you have four leaders reporting to you who are better than you in key areas. I like to say that you can disappear for a given area for six months and no one will care. That's a +4. Without it, you can only scale yourself so far, and that is frustrating.

You are smart; your positioning isn't. Since you deliver all the solutions, you can articulate them perfectly. But you haven't spent equal time to position, package, and articulate your offering so anyone can sell it.

You operate with low trust. Your default is to protect your pond, so you look at partners as people who might mess up your business. You tend to trust external partners more easily than internal partners, since you know they are less threatening. You imagine how they might take your business or take over the client relationship. Your mind assesses the negatives.

You won't let go. Of anything. Part of your self-worth is tied up in your ability to control your offering or firm. If you let go, ironically, you'll start to grow. If you don't let go, you just limit the amount of oxygen you will have to grow.

My recommendation to those of us who find ourselves fighting small pond syndrome is to plan out what you are willing to do. Think of the easiest decisions to the hardest and write out a plan for the next twelve, twenty-four, and thirty-six months. And then methodically execute against your plan.

When we are stuck in this mindset, we don't just change. Rather, we need to teach ourselves, step by step, that evolving our approach will lead to more success, even if every move we make isn't successful. We learn to trust that this has been done before.

We can get there if we are willing to look in the mirror and accept that it is actually ourselves that are creating the issues we face.

And that gets back to our quote. Think of what you fear and start thinking that this may be your indicator that it is what you should consider doing. Maybe Ralph Waldo Emerson was right after all.

CHAPTER 74

HOW TO FRAME A COLUMN—PART 1

"The thought process can never be complete without articulation."

—Stephen King

Many of us talk about doing more thought leadership, writing columns, and expressing our views.

I have found that a simple way to do this, when possible, is to outline a series of insights, so that the reader can pick up on a series of ideas rather than just one.

In general, focus on a finite set of insights, usually three to five or ten, but nothing in between. Ask yourself if each insight will get your peers to think about it for a second. If yes, you are on the right track.

Here is an example of a column I wrote for *PR Newswire*:

COLUMN

The work of bad actors is no longer a curiosity for journalists and communications leaders. The toxic brew of security, public health, and privacy risks demand the development of a new discipline within PR and new models for journalism.

Here are a few of the most important trends and ideas I shared recently during a keynote (January 9, 2022) for the National Press Foundation to bolster this point.

Trust is evolving, not decreasing. It is only partially correct to state that trust is plummeting for businesses, government, and other institutions. Trust is simultaneously increasing for social media influencers. The majority of the world receives their information via social channels and search engines. With attention spans of just one to three seconds, we become fixated on certain people within certain channels, leading to an Instagram, YouTube, or TikTok influencer having more weight in our minds than a traditional media outlet. We develop trust with those who we interact with daily.

Disinformation is a highly disciplined effort. It's time to stop thinking disinformation is someone else's problem. It is increasingly sophisticated. In fact, we like to say the best disinformation looks like information, and it takes many forms. For example, I worry the most about software that can create stories in seconds. It's 95 percent accurate. A bad actor just changes one quote or fact. If you want to disinform an audience for the long term, this is a great way to do it.

Censorship occurs every day. Every algorithm has a human behind it. Humans have organizations behind them. Sometimes that organization has a country beyond it. The result is censorship is occurring in ways we don't appreciate. For example, imagine that you criticize an approach government X is taking. Soon after, your content is suppressed by the platform's algorithm, and your videos shift from an average of ten thousand views to one thousand views. You've been shadow banned. If caught, the platform will surely say, "Oops, we didn't realize it." This is just one technique most of us are not fully aware of.

Organized crime is rampant online. Ransomware is a business. Counterfeit products and services are a business. Illegal drugs and human trafficking are a business. Organized crime loves the digital world and invests time and resources to figure out how to expose every weakness we exhibit online.

We have an obligation to protect our companies, the brands we provide to our customers, and the citizens we ultimately serve.

So, what do we do?

Journalists need to get out of the newsroom and into the social room. The number one reason why social media influencers succeed is that they personalize the content they deliver. Imagine if a journalist delivered their content directly onto Facebook, YouTube, or Instagram every day. We would bond with those journalists. Traditional media is viewed as too impersonal by the majority of the world, unfortunately. Build the bond every day, person to person. One to many.

We need to rethink listening platforms. Platforms that tell us all the wonderful things we are doing are nice to have. Intelligence platforms are next. New ones will outline how ransomware gangs are working and which trolls and bots are actively disinforming us about the Ukraine/Russia war and expose the media models of bad actors who are actively recruiting individuals to their cause, whether it is a white supremacist group or an adversarial country.

Intelligence platforms will utilize the 1:9:90 media model in quite a different way.

Let's use disinformation as an example. We can easily figure out who the 1 percent are who are creating the disinformation. What we are not as good at is figuring out who is helping to move the disinformation, either on purpose or unwittingly, to reach a wider audience. And, to reach the majority of us, the passive 90 percent who utilize search engines to answer questions or social media channels to learn, we must become fluent in how to decrease the impact of disinformation.

Today's leader must understand search engine optimization and the 1:9:90 model if they hope to understand and slow down the impact of disinformation.

We need to stop being embarrassed about being hacked. The main leverage ransomware gangs have is that our companies don't want public awareness of the breach. If we all talked openly about this problem, their leverage would greatly decrease, their prices would drop, and they would have to find new ways to hassle us.

We need to consider utilizing "technology for good" as a new social purpose model. What if we applied our intellect to protecting our citizens, communities, companies, and countries? It would make a major difference, and it is quantifiable.

Lastly, we end with a warning for those who stretch moral boundaries and a reminder that we will find those who try to take advantage of our digital world.

Think of it this way. If we can figure out who in St. Petersburg, Russia, is part of a certain ransomware gang, we're fairly sure we can find you if you are choosing to disinform here in the US.

Having a strong ethical center is more important than ever. Detecting and publicly discussing those who censor matters. Exposing those who disinform and showing how they do it matters. And on the positive side, learning from those who succeed in digital media and then adopting their playbook matters.

Seth Godin once said, "The job isn't to catch up to the status quo; the job is to invent the status quo."

Well said. Let's make it happen.

CHAPTER 75

LOGICAL THINKING DRIVES THE LOGIC OF TECHNOLOGY

"Logic will get you from A to B.
Imagination will take you everywhere."
— *unknown*

Software and algorithms and creative positioning make a big difference in our lives, but this workflow is only as strong as our ability to realize it is better together, not separate.

It is why we often describe the best programmers and data scientists as the "new creatives." It's easy to build an app or an algorithm. It's difficult to build something that creates unique advantage in the marketplace. And it is equally difficult to position a new idea, so it sells "effortlessly."

I have found that the best first step for those who think of ideas for a living is to focus on what we do well.

Identify the problem or opportunity. Figure out what you want to accomplish. And then partner with software engineers, data scientists, and creatives to figure out your next steps.

The breakthroughs occur when we learn how to all work together. Really very similar to how we learn to work with the top creative minds in our business. We have to learn (and respect) how we each think and figure out how to talk to each other.

Learning how to speak to each other is the key point.

Let's take a simple example to illustrate the point.

I ask a data science, software programmer, and creative to help us think through how to build a new platform that will enable us to see how physicians learn online and understand how their behavior is shaped. Right now, it is just an idea written on a whiteboard in between meetings.

The data scientists start thinking about where we will obtain this information, how accessible the data sources are, and how we can build scraping mechanisms to gain this data earlier. Then we need to walk over to the software programmers.

The software programmers are wondering how they can automate our ability to find more than one million medical providers to learn from. They are wondering how we will build this platform and scale it and where the data should be housed in the cloud, who will write the code, and more, while the creatives are already brainstorming in a different way.

The creatives are tossing out the name of the platform. They are sketching out a rough architecture of how it will look and imagining how we will introduce it to the general public.

If we all learn to respect our thinking processes, this is magic. If we believe our way of thinking is the right way and everyone else is out of order, well, we are not going anywhere.

The punch line is that all three of these groups are creative. It takes real ingenuity to understand how to find and harness data or build a platform that can scale or brand it in a manner that everyone wants to learn more about. They do not have to go in order.

Learn how your colleagues think. Understand how they process information. And be respectful of the time they need to solve problems. If you do this and openly discuss it, you will build a creative approach that is unmatched. If you don't, well, you are just like everyone else.

No one ever said breakthroughs were easy. Take the time to understand how to build a next-generation creative team.

LEADERSHIP INSIGHT

Thoughtful Leaders Become Thought Leaders

You have ideas to contribute and learnings to share.

Don't keep them to yourself. Share them.

In doing so, you learn how to express your thinking publicly, so that it can influence and inspire others to share their ideas or perhaps imagine new ways to work. It's a great way to test how strong your ideas really are.

If you love your profession, what a way to give back.

If you are learning your profession, what a great way to gain feedback.

If you are learning about new areas, you want to find the right people to listen to.

My view is we have an obligation as leaders to share what we know.

With this in mind, I now share several columns I have written to illustrate what I mean.

CHAPTER 76

HOW TO FRAME A COLUMN—PART 2

"Complexity is your enemy.
Any fool can make something complicated.
It is hard to keep things simple."
—*Richard Branson*

WHY RANSOMWARE DESERVES OUR ATTENTION

I find that many aspects of society are addressed by people who are deep experts who thrive in complexities. It is their way of speaking, represents their comfort level, and leaves most of us in the dust.

How many times have we thought, "Wow, he/she is smart, but I am not sure what they said." My view is that smart people often hide behind complexity, rather than taking the time to make it simple.

Richard Branson is one of the masters of making anything sound far simpler than it is. It has led to his personal branding as a leader that can do anything. Airline? Sure. Record company? Why not.

Take time to go deep on chronic issues facing all of us, so you can talk about the topic in a way that a college student or an entry-level team member can understand. If you do this, you will actually reach far more people in the C-suite, who also don't understand, but don't want to admit it.

Here is an example:

This was written for the Page Turner blog to reach communications professionals. This example is a post written with two colleagues after we participated in a webinar together.

BLOG POST

It is not a big surprise that the first episode of ransomware in the world of technology occurred in the same year, 1989, Tim Berners-Lee designed the plan for the worldwide web.

In the next thirty-two years, we have seen ransomware evolve from personal attacks to highly sophisticated organized crime gangs that have built a new economic model, Ransomware as a Service or RaaS, that rivals the best software companies coming out of Silicon Valley.

Their areas of focus remind us of the famous quote by the bank robber Willie Sutton, who was asked why he robs banks. His answer was, "Because that's where the money is."

For ransomware gangs, that translates into the wealthier countries of our world and specific industries believed to be less secure. Based on actual ransomware attacks in the last thirty days, Professional Services is the lead industry, followed by Internet Software and Services, Construction and Engineering, and Education Services. Other industries are not far behind.

We often wonder how hackers get into our systems. Security experts know there are well over two hundred common ways to breach our systems.

The good news is we know a decent amount about who is conducting these attacks. About eight organized groups lead most attacks on our organizations. We know where they are based. We can figure out their modus operandi, ranging from how they attack us to what types of requests they routinely make for ransom. We know they are often inside our organizations for up to 280 days before they alert us. And more.

The question is what we can do to improve, which was the subject of our webinar today.

We start by taking these organizations seriously. They are technically proficient, smart, and savvy about how to extract value from us, and they are counting on us to be filled with surprise, fear, and anxiety that causes us to panic and pay their ransom request.

Here are six actions we can take to prepare and get ready to represent our interests more effectively.

First, we improve our listening/intelligence of bad actors. Imagine our current listening platform tells us what is happening related to our organization. Now, add to it social channels, forums, additional search engines, and key areas of the dark web to our listening profile, so we can now watch how bad actors plan, act, recruit, and go about their business.

Second, we can develop new red team scenarios, where we learn how to prepare, negotiate, and take appropriate action. We must remember that we are dealing with criminals, not activists. The rules of engagement are different. And we should red team in advance, so our leaders do not react emotionally in the throes of an attack.

Third, we need to band together to find, track, and expose bad actors. We should share our learnings with peer companies privately, so we can all learn closer to real time how ransomware is occurring. We need to improve what we can provide to authorities to make it easier for them to pursue justice.

Fourth, we should always think through in advance who we will need to contact, including our customers, legal authorities in key states, federal authorities, law enforcement, our board, our employees, and more. The cadence of how we do this can be as important as the message since these scenarios often play out in private for days or even weeks.

Fifth, we should be ready to negotiate or even say no. Bad actors can't make money unless our organizations or insurance companies pay. Once they try to sell our data, we have an easier chance of locating them.

And finally, we need to all be supportive of each other and realize any organization can be targeted. We should not be embarrassed or ashamed. We should not try to sweep the issue under the rug.

The bad actors of our world are hoping we stay fragmented, don't share our learnings, and are filled with fear and anxiety about what could happen.

If we don't give them that satisfaction and band together, share our learnings, and prepare in advance to represent our interests, we have taken one of the key steps towards minimizing their impact.

Technology doesn't change the crime. It just changes the approach and the sophistication of the criminal.

And with that knowledge, it is equally important we evolve with the world we live in.

CHAPTER 77

HOW TO MEMORIALIZE A DISCUSSION

"Leadership is influence."

—*John C. Maxwell*

You were just asked to speak at an industry conference. You prepare and are now on stage with two other leaders to talk about the future of something for thirty minutes. It takes five minutes to get started, one of your panelists is long-winded, and the moderator ends by saying, "Well, that was great. Wish we had time for questions," and you end. You walk away feeling like you sort of contributed, but had a lot more to offer.

The audience had one hundred or two hundred people in it who listened that day.

This talk was simply your springboard to share your full thoughts via a post or videocast where you articulate your thinking and share it via LinkedIn or other social channels.

What you are doing is "memorializing" your thinking. Now, your ideas can be found via search. You can include them on your website. They are a forever reference point on how you think.

The example below is a great example. A fun webinar that probably reached thirty to fifty people that day. Yet, our post reached thousands a day later and continues to receive visits.

If we believe leadership is influence, then we need to ensure that our thinking has the opportunity to influence.

The easiest way to think of it is when the webinar ends or the podcast concludes, your outreach is now ready to begin, not end.

DISCUSSING OUR "INFODEMIC" AS PART OF A PRSA WEBINAR SERIES

On Tuesday, November 16, I joined Vivian Schiller and moderator Jim O'Leary to discuss our current "infodemic" for a PRSA webinar titled "A Communicator's Strategic and Tactical Guide to Disinformation and Digital Protection."

Vivian has extensive media experience, whether as president/CEO of NPR, head of news for Twitter, or her current role as executive director at the Aspen Institute. And as you know, I teach, counsel, and innovate with the private and public sector on how we improve our ability to combat disinformation worldwide.

Here are seven key learnings from our webinar:

#1 – We are experiencing a long-term infodemic. Whether we think of Russia disinforming us about Covid-19, how white supremacists try to recruit, or how adversaries distort the truth in any venue, disinformation is here to stay. We should assume that bad actors will increase their capabilities. We are in a race to understand what to do and how to diminish their impact.

#2 – Avoid the "data void." When an organization has a small digital footprint, your risk is far higher if you are attacked with disinformation. Think of a simple Google search. If your company or brand is showing up with twenty thousand or two hundred thousand results when you do a search query, you are at high risk. The best defense is a great offense. Tell your story widely, use the right keywords, and create density for your top search queries, so you have two million results, not twenty thousand. Think of it as a digital insurance policy.

#3 – Expertise in understanding bad actors is a fundamental skill required of leaders today. Every chief communications officer and their team should understand three important areas of intelligence: a) who is disparaging your company/brand/leaders, b) which antagonists are going against your company and how do they plan/act online, and c) which criminals are likely to attack your company and how do you track them, e.g., ransomware, counterfeits, IP theft.

#4—"Countering" disinformation is not the answer. When you counter a person or group, you are telling them they are incorrect. This irritates the person/group, makes them more determined, and usually exacerbates the situation. Think of what happens when you tell a teenager not to do something. We're all wired that way. The answer is not to counter, but to build a powerful narrative, tell our story in the right places, use the right keywords, and outmaneuver bad actors. Strategic communication is the answer. Be smarter than our adversaries, not combative.

#5—We will shift from listening to intelligence platforms. Social media listening platforms continue to serve a purpose. Just imagine their insights as one-half of what you need. The other half is understanding who is against you, who is dissatisfied, and what you can learn about them. This can help with a range of organizational needs, including improving customer experience, preparing for an activist attack, or slowing down the counterfeiting of your most important goods and services. We are really redefining how we look at crisis/issues management and how we prepare for the future via an intelligence platform that educates us, helps us prepare, and more.

#6—Study the future to understand how to prepare. We know now that we can build content into blocks, enabling one person to create hundreds or thousands of posts, videos, and audio clips in any language. This 1:30 model is new but will be mainstream before we know it. I'm an adviser to a company that can do this today, as an example. As communicators, how many of us are exploring this technology now or other breakthroughs? And this is the point. Focus on the next three to five key technologies that will evolve our function and be ready to utilize them for good uses. If you don't know what they are, ask and learn how to keep up with what's next.

#7 – Check out the Aspen Institute for more info. The Aspen Institute is providing excellent information related to our infodemic. There is a continual flow of education and insights from leaders that are worth your time.

Overall, let's view this moment as one where we can take a fresh look at how we protect our organization's reputation. It is time for us to redefine how we prepare and conduct for issues, crises, and more. The old way might keep us out of the headlines, but it doesn't solve the problem. It's the start, not the finish.

Our companies, communities, citizens, and even our country are counting on us.

CHAPTER 78

THE UNFINISHED BUSINESS OF HEALTHCARE

"It is health that is real wealth and not pieces of gold and silver."

—*Mahatma Gandhi*

When we are listening to our peers discuss their thinking, we look for perspective and anecdotes that will resonate with each of us. We are the audience, and the audience always looks to align.

In writing about a sector, like healthcare, it's important to go beyond the offering you have and reflect on the passion we all share about this particular area. Our passion comes through when we link the facts of a disease or disorder with the people who are battling it.

If we are passionate about an area, let it show. Don't let other people "perfect" your thinking. Be yourself and say what is likely on the minds of those who are reading along with you. And, when possible, enable your peers to share their stories as well. After all, it always takes a team to do anything significant, and in areas like healthcare, that team is a big one.

Here is an example from *O'Dwyers:*

Column

The healthcare industry is a deeply personal place to work.

Over 95 percent of the world's population has health problems.

An average of 1,905 people die of heart disease in the US every day.

There are more than seven thousand rare diseases.

It is a list that can quickly become overwhelming. It is hard to comprehend. But what is not difficult to understand is what it means to each individual battling disease.

Our team has talked with people dying of disease who still remain optimistic about how medicine may impact the next generation.

We have talked with countless family members whose only questions revolve around, "What can we do?"

And we have witnessed the frustration of these same people and their care circle who can't gain access in time for a treatment, either due to the pace of the approval process or a lack of reimbursement.

Today is what matters to everyone battling a disease or disorder. Tomorrows are what they desire to have. Really, what we all desire to have.

In healthcare, we serve as their agents of change.

And this is why we are excited about the future of healthcare.

The capabilities of science are unlocking the personalization of medicine at an unprecedented rate, driven by rare diseases, the emergence of gene-based therapies, the continued impact of immunotherapy, and our growing ability to edit genes via CRISPR.

This is resulting in diagnostic and treatment solutions we could not have imagined a decade ago.

For decades, tractor trailers have pulled up to the US Food and Drug Administration to drop off their New Drug Application (NDA), but now we can and should deliver all this information via the cloud. The cloud and related technologies are finally giving us opportunities to transform everything from drug development to how we learn about and protect our own health.

Our ability to collapse time to market is a game changer.

The third driver—payment for treatment and services—needs to evolve with the same pace so that we can benefit from scientific and technological advance.

If incentives are aligned with what we can deliver, we'll improve health outcomes.

The nice thing about technological advances is that they normally drive costs down, not up, so we are hopeful this can also translate into healthcare as well.

What's our mission?

It's about making a difference for individuals fighting for their health and their families.

Our goal is to improve compliance, expand the "office," accelerate drug development, and build powerful narratives that make it more obvious as to why government, science, and industry can move in lockstep.

So, what does that mean? Well, here are a few examples.

Imagine accelerating the development of treatments.

New analytic models can analyze all the published literature for a particular therapeutic area for the past ten years in minutes with new insights in hours. Analytics can show us which investigators have been most effective in enrolling in clinical trials for that same time period.

This can tell us which investigators are best to select to enroll in a trial. We can determine how to communicate the new characteristics of a treatment, so that it aligns with the evolution of the category and reaches providers and payors at the earliest possible stage. Precision in trial design. Precision in who runs trials. Precision in the scientific narrative.

We can complete trials faster with better enrollment, leading to a faster time to market. Once on the market, we can accelerate access via improved evidence-based communication. We'll focus on both areas.

Once a treatment is on the market, we have plenty of issues to deal with. Compliance is one.

It is estimated that between 33-69 percent of all medication-related hospital admissions in the US are due to poor medication adherence, costing the US about $100 billion annually. Yet, we have technology today that can teach patients, in real time, how to use an asthma inhaler, rather than waiting for that same patient to have a failure and end up in the hospital. Imagine our son or daughter trying to use an asthma inhaler at home. Wouldn't they prefer to learn via a video on their phone and talk with someone in real time? It's how they do everything else anyway, right?

Technology makes it easier to teach patients how to improve their health right in their home.

We'll embrace technologies that align with how we use them every day for new uses to improve our health. Common sense.

We will help with paradigm shifts. If we work in a hybrid world where it is normal to conduct our work in both an office and at home with similar results, why can't healthcare do the same?

Many agree. The global telehealth market is estimated at $89 billion in 2022 and is expected to grow to $787 billion by 2028. This is a *major* growth market, but it will only find its rightful place if physicians and nurses are reimbursed properly and payors can see that a virtual visit can be as good or better than an office visit.

What's the real difference if our health can be improved?

It is easy to cast blame if new advances in science and technology are not utilized, but that's not our orientation. We believe that building a convincing narrative matters. Understanding how the Audience Architecture interacts related to a disease matters. Knowing how technology works and being able to explain it is important. Knowing how to build analytics models and use AI is now a mainstream need of agencies like ours today.

We see a world where the rapid growth of personalized treatments, as well as those for rare conditions, requires that our media models also become highly personalized and have the ability to adjust to smaller market sizes.

We realize disease-based media modeling, which is highly customized to a community's needs, represents the future of PESO (paid, earned, shared, owned) media planning. After all, we live in a world that is more of a series of neighborhoods rather than one big place.

We see a new style of creative brief that includes AI-driven insights that we didn't have last year or even last quarter.

It is our job to innovate in the world of communications to match up with the advances in science and technology.

It is also our job to remember the conversations we have had with people battling disease and disorder and their families who are searching for solutions when we are working late at night or traveling on the weekend and embrace our unique ability to make a difference in the world via our actions.

We end with a simple and powerful story from our past.

Many years ago, an accomplished business executive from Maryland called us up while we were working in a pharmaceutical company. His wife had ALS, and he wanted to learn more.

A few weeks later, he drove up, unannounced, to our office in Pennsylvania. We welcomed him, and he entered our office to ask a series of questions.

We were ready to answer many more questions when he abruptly stopped.

What he said we will never forget.

> *I came up here to judge if you care about developing this drug and making a difference. I now have no question in my mind this is the case. Thank you for everything you are doing for my wife, our family, and all the other families who suffer from this disease. Let me now let you get back to work. I wish you the best of luck.*

He then shook our hands, walked out, and returned to his home in Maryland, never to be heard from again. Yet, he will be remembered forever.

We did successfully launch this drug, which was the first drug ever approved for ALS. We did it in full partnership with the ALS community and their families, and although it was a struggle to gain approval, we never wavered.

It is conversations like this and the trust that we know people place in all of us that motivates us even at the most frustrating moments.

We have unfinished business in healthcare.

Our answer is to form a new healthcare team across The Bliss Group and The Next Practices Group called NPG Health, which will launch later this year.

CHAPTER 79

WHAT TECHNOLOGY ACCOMPLISHES IS UP TO US

"Every once in a while, a new technology, an old problem and a big idea turn into an innovation."

—Dean Kamen

This is a second column, also written for *O'Dwyers*, on technology. This column is meant to portray an attitude we have about technology. It is why we are excited about how technology can impact every square inch of our world. Our goal is to get that across in this column.

We assume the reader knows we do all the stuff you would expect consultants to do. Do we really need to constantly remind each other of our full offering? Can it get more boring?

Instead, share your attitude. Share your point of view. Share your passion.

Here is the column:

Technology makes our dreams come alive. It allows us to remove barriers in our brains and imagine how a solution might come about. It leads us to think about a world without a need for passwords.

It makes us wonder why all our healthcare information can't be available to us in a personalized cloud…today.

It inspires us to think about how technology can democratize who can access it and build a successful business, often with far less cash than needed in the past. It helps us learn from friends anywhere in the world.

Technology is inspiring, and it's why we are focused on building a technology practice that empowers entrepreneurs to achieve their dreams through the use of technology.

We realize that transformational changes in society require us to keep up with their progress. In our world, it means we are always learning how technologies work, such as blockchain, or taking the time to understand how an entire field, like artificial intelligence, can be used in myriad ways.

We also realize that any technology, in the wrong hands, can cause trouble, leading to an increase in cybercrime, ransomware, counterfeiting and countless new ways to steal, disinform and wreak havoc.

Our team has a responsibility to provide an offering that promotes new technologies and protects us from their use by bad actors.

We live in a fascinating time. A time where an app we never heard of became the fastest-growing app in history and is now the most visited site in the world. We know it as TikTok.

A time where Goldman Sachs now has 12,000 engineers, or one of every four employees.

The list of amazing technology-related advances and investments can go on forever, it seems, but that's actually not what gets us the most excited.

Our team loves speaking with entrepreneurs who share their vision for the future and ask us to be part of the solution to ensure their audience knows and understands what is possible.

We know that money fuels technology advance, which is why we are focused on partnering with companies in their journey from an idea to an IPO and beyond.

Being in technology for decades, we realize that a technological advance doesn't mean anyone automatically cares. Every advance requires a narrative that does it justice in explaining how the technology works and why it is valuable.

Technology unlocks us and we unlock it.

What is equally fascinating about technology is how it evolves how we work in incremental steps that may initially sound mundane but are arguably revolutionary.

Understanding the history of how technology evolves informs the present. Dale Laszig, who writes the Street Smarts column for [the Green Sheet], said it best when she recently reflected on how "the password-less journey in payments requires the same guiding principles that informed early hardware designs."

Understanding the economic cycles that impact technology's advance is also critical, particularly related to valuation. Gregory Bedrosian, Managing Partner and CEO of Drake Star Partners, said, "Before the downturn, people were asking me to be introduced to technology companies that were changing the world. Today, they are asking to be introduced to companies that are EBIDTA positive."

A change in how we value companies also deserves a change in how we tell their story.

Our media models are designed to reach the right people within the 5.5 billion people who are online today. Our job is to make it simple to reach our core audience in a world where we have seven billion Google searches a day and view videos 6.5 billion times daily. The world may be increasingly complex, which is why our analytics-driven media models must be increasingly clear and scalable.

And about those billions of people, we never forget that we have an obligation to utilize technology in a manner that is responsible and, when possible, addresses societal problems in new ways.

Our team has expertise in how to combat misinformation and disinformation, so that we can diminish or even avoid its impact. We believe that building a reputation in today's society requires equal skill in defending it via the most recent uses of technology, including expertise in the deep and dark web.

We live in a world that is battling issues, ranging from climate change to malnutrition. It's why we're going big in building a purpose-driven offering that can help leaders imagine how their technology can drive revenue for shareholders and opportunities for citizens of our world.

Technology will always transform society as we know it.

What matters is how we apply it to make a difference.

It's why we wake up every morning imagining how our clients will contribute to improving our world. Our vehicle to help them includes media relations, brand positioning and all the things you would expect across communications, public affairs and marketing.

When our day ends, we ask ourselves if we are making a difference through our support of some of the smartest technology entrepreneurs in the world.

It's a question that will never end and never gets old.

CHAPTER 80

OUR FUTURE

"Management is doing things right;
leadership is doing the right things."

—Peter Drucker

If you have read this book, you are likely someone fortunate to have an opportunity to shape your future and those of your team.

Every minute is precious. Every day provides opportunities to impact others. Every year holds new surprises. Every client assignment represents a new chance to innovate.

We are filled with ideas and aspirations, which leads me to my final thoughts for *Firm Beliefs.*

Don't let the noise distract you. Don't listen to the naysayers.

Don't limit your own potential. Don't get too comfortable too quickly in your career.

It is my belief that we all hold more value inside us than we realize. It can impact people's lives, and it's a lot of fun to find out what we're capable of really doing.

Make that commitment. For you. No one else.

Succeed and fail. Learn and listen. And identify, reinforce, and continually develop your own firm beliefs, the ones that will make a difference in your life.

Thanks for joining me on this journey.

AFTERWORD

THOUGHTS ON HOW TO UTILIZE THIS BOOK

"Common sense is not so common."

— *Voltaire*

If we are candid with ourselves, we realize that much of life involves the application of common sense. Most solutions are so easy to figure out once we try that we are astonished at how we didn't think of them before.

Yet, those who choose to reflect and relearn and keep applying the equivalent of a mirror to their professional lives are the ones who succeed most often. Don't make excuses or procrastinate or talk too much or engage in one of the many shields to avoid dealing with common sense.

This book is meant to be a reference you can open, reflect on a chapter, rethink an insight, and then move forward.

Keep it nearby.

People who want to unlock continually learn.

Imagine your career like climbing a mountain range. Sometimes it is fairly easy. Sometimes you take the wrong path. Other times it is just exhausting. But you keep making progress, and it is rewarding as you reach new levels in your climb.

It's that journey that really never ends.

ACKNOWLEDGMENTS

Everything in life that has been meaningful to me has involved a team.

I am thankful for the mentors I have had and still have in my career. They are too numerous to mention, but I'll mention a few.

My mom and dad taught me how to play sports, be a good team member, learn how to practice, accept and learn from loss, and so many lessons that have all applied to life, personally and professionally.

My Little League baseball team, the Eagles, was coached by Harvey McMann, Joe Cohn, and Larry Berezin, who taught us how to be good sports, not just to be good at the sport.

I am thankful to Bill Heyman, who has been a guide throughout my career, helping me figure out what's next. Bill helped me learn how to dream professionally from the time I was a twenty-three-year-old wondering if I should jump into the pharmaceutical industry through today.

David Catlett, Liz Moench, Katherine Coughlin, and Cathy Kernen believed that a young kid could somehow learn how to launch brands in the pharmaceutical industry. They taught me the craft of product marketing and how to have the confidence to go with it.

Merritt Allen and Sam Gibbons taught me what it means to get up every day and learn how to sell, even if those we sold to could care less if we showed up in some cases. Merritt and Sam taught me the power of sales and discipline and focusing on what you do when no one is watching.

Liz Moench propelled me forward when she made a bet on me to become a director at Rhône-Poulenc Rorer at a relatively young age. Steve Kelmar did the same years later when I took on a new role at Novartis.

Christophe Bianchi, Herve Hoppenot, Jean-Jacques Bienaime, Joe Scodari, Joanna Horobin, Thierry Soursac, Arvind Sood, Tim Rothwell, Steve Downs, Joe Caminiti, Pat Barbera, Frank Fila, Joe Papa, Mike Kishbauch, Gary Freedman and so many others at Rhône-Poulenc Rorer and CIBA-GEIGY showed me what it takes to build great brands, often purely through their actions.

Bob Feldman was the first person to believe I could be an entrepreneur when he asked me to build GCI Health from scratch. It was Bob's support that enabled me to think I could really do it. This is where I also met a generation of leaders I still work with today, such as Ray Kerins, Jr. and Michael Roth.

Jim Weiss was the next person to imagine that we could be better together, and that path took us on a journey to build what is now Real Chemistry. So many people within this firm helped me see things differently due to their creativity and counseling ability, including Paulo Simas, Gary Grates, and Jennifer Gottlieb. The list is too long, but you know who you are. And today, I continue to innovate with many of these leaders within our current firm, including Colin Foster and Yash Gad.

Kip Knight and Ed Tazzia welcomed me to teach at the US State Department years ago to share what I was learning in the private sector. Many years later, I continue to teach and learn from the most patriotic people on earth.

I find myself blessed to have had the opportunity to learn from Rob Cawthorn and Michel de Rosen, who led Rhône-Poulenc Rorer, Dan Vasella, who led Novartis, and Michael Dell. Watching how they operate at the global CEO level was like getting another MBA. I also benefited by watching Marc Benioff work his magic in the early days of Salesforce.com. You can learn so much just by observing and reflecting.

Dave Bixel and Bill Cunningham showed Donna and I the value of giving our time and resources to support those in need, which has shaped our view of philanthropy.

And today, the leaders of The Next Practices Group are my mentors, peers, and friends who inspire me to think ahead, once again, to team up and make a difference. I want to thank Cortney Stapleton and Michael Roth for often saying, "That should be in the book," as we went about our days, addressing opportunities and issues. Many of those moments are, indeed, captured in *Firm Beliefs*.

The biggest lesson I have learned is the insights for leadership are right in front of us. We just have to be observant enough to see them. Thank you to this team and many more leaders who have been special parts of my life.

The team theme continues with the creation of this book.

I am thankful to TLC Graphics, Tami Dever, Monica Thomas, and Misti Moyer, who make each book come alive from the cover to the look and feel of the book itself. It is their passion for creating books that inspires me, in part, to write the next one.

I end with the ultimate team. My family.

The only reason I have been able to work like I have, learn from others, and then share these insights is due to their support. Without it, none of this happens, so any accomplishments I have are truly shared. Any failures, well, that's on me.

Our two daughters, Nicole and Brittany, have heard some of these insights over the years and are now finding how true they are in their own lives. Nicole as a paralegal and mom, and Brittany in her work in marketing, marriage to Sam Rivoli, and pursuit of an MBA, while Sam completes dental school at Creighton.

We have learned as a family, lived overseas, experienced what it is like to join a new company, start a new company, and go through the ups and downs of all of it. When I say ups and downs, we have had our share in life, personal and professional, and what we have learned is how we deal with adversity really does define us, shape us, and make us grateful that we have the opportunity to love life, work hard, and have fun.

Our family is shaped by this journey we are taking together.

The best way to close is to say thank you to my wife, Donna. We have been married for thirty-four years, and she has been supportive of me since day one. As two kids who grew up in New Jersey with what we called, "lots of love, but not much money," we are the lucky ones. Not because we ended up doing well, but because we had parents who cared about us. The original team.

It is part of the attraction of life that we spend so much of our time figuring it out.

Best,

Bob

July 2023

NEXT STEPS & NEW IDEAS

When an insight leads you to think of a personal action, jot down the idea and the page number here.

NEXT STEPS & NEW IDEAS

NEXT STEPS & NEW IDEAS

NEXT STEPS & NEW IDEAS

NEXT STEPS & NEW IDEAS

Bob Pearson is the author of *Pre-Commerce* and *Storytizing* and co-author of *Countering Hate* and *Crafting Persuasion*. He is Chair of The Next Practices Group, a teacher for The University of Texas at Austin McCombs School of Business and for the US government, and an adviser and investor for both technology and purpose-led companies. He has led global communications for several Fortune 500 companies. Bob resides in Austin, Texas, with his wife, Donna.

Printed in the USA
CPSIA information can be obtained
at www.ICGtesting.com
LVHW021937250823
756272LV00030B/1032/J

9 798988 23150